PABLO HELGUERA

WHAT IN THE WORLD

A MUSEUM'S SUBJECTIVE BIOGRAPHY

Jorge Pinto Books Inc.
New York

WHAT IN THE WORLD

A Project for Philagrafika 2010

PHILAGRAfiKA 2010

Cover design: Pablo Helguera
Book design: Charles King, website: www.ckmm.com

ISBN-10:1-934978-28-0
ISBN-13: 978-1-934978-28-3

Para Estela

quien me deletrea

Contents

Introduction

THROUGHOUT THE TWENTY or so years I have worked in the education departments of art museums, I have gradually become interested the biographical anecdotes, oral histories, and archived or nearly forgotten stories—most of which are seldom visible or communicated to the public—about the generations of collectors, directors, curators, and educators whose vision and interests have shaped the nature and tone of the institutions and their collections. This book contains a small group of biographical divertimentos connected to a museum with a particularly remarkable trove of such stories.

Most museums have a mission of educating through object-centered study, firm in the nineteenth-century belief that an object is a microcosm of a culture or an artwork a window to the world of an artist. What this focus often underplays is the fact that there are usually very subjective reasons—philosophical, personal, political—for the presence of an object or artwork at a particular museum, reasons why it was chosen by a specific person to represent a particular culture or art movement (or, conversely, why certain objects or artworks are absent).

In other words, what are often missing in the story of an artifact are the crucial histories not of its maker but of those who brought it to the museum—the objects' "curatorial parents"— and of those who created the interpretive frameworks that envelop objects as they are absorbed into museum collections. The State Hermitage Museum's collection can't be explained without Peter the Great, in the same way that the Solomon R. Guggenheim Museum, the Frick Collection, and the Isabella Stewart Gardner

Museum owe the peculiarities of their collections to their founders. But while founders usually leave their names on the door of an institution, the hands of its curators are less prominent and most of them are forgotten after a generation or two.

Sometimes this alternative, people-driven history is unexceptional or irrelevant and sometimes it is unsavory or even embarrassing, but it often is useful and even illuminating, shedding light on the ideas and values that prevailed when the collection was created.

Of all American cities, Philadelphia has perhaps the most illustrious history in the early era of museum visionaries. Pierre Eugene du Simitiere opened his coin collection to the public under the name American Museum in 1782 in Philadelphia, and a few years later Charles Willson Peale opened the first natural history museum (also the first major museum institution) in the United States there. As one of the historically key centers for science in the United States, Philadelphia has a history of strange collections. In 1858 Dr. Thomas Dent Mütter donated his collection of medical oddities to the College of Physicians of Philadelphia, creating the Mütter Museum.

It is against this historical background that the University of Pennsylvania Museum of Archaeology and Anthropology emerged in the late nineteenth century. In the words of historian Steven Conn, the University Museum was "amongst the first institutions in this country—and probably the most ambitious—to create a separate space, both physically and intellectually, for the display of human artifacts apart from collections of natural history or specimens. Proposed by the University provost [William

Pepper] as early as 1889, the University Museum, when it moved from temporary quarters to its new home in 1899, tried to do what the Peabody [Museum of Natural History, Yale University,] and the Field [Museum, Chicago,] had not yet done—occupy the space between science and art."[1] Aside from its central place in the history of American culture, the University Museum is a unique example of how individuals connected to a museum can leave a significant mark on the institution. The unusual cast of characters that formed the museum and helped give it shape during its first half-century of life run the gamut of eccentricity, ambition, idealism, and even melodrama.

Thus the University Museum is, I think, an ideal candidate for such an examination of its personalities through its collection. Its galleries and its objects are a collection of two tales: the one of the ancient culture that the curators sought to tell, and the unintended story of themselves and their vision.

In the same way that museums have two stories, this book is a doubly subjective biography of the University Museum. On the one hand, it is an attempt to show how the personal interests and obsessions of certain individuals influenced the life of the museum; on the other hand, it is my own subjective focus on a selected group of people that, to me, represent interesting aspects of curating, collecting, exhibiting, and interpreting that are common to most museums.

It should be pointed out that, seen through the prism of time, the subjects of these stories may appear at times naïve,

---

1. Steven Conn, *Museums and American Intellectual Life, 1876–1926* (Chicago: University of Chicago Press, 1998), p. 83.

egotistical, and messianic. It is important to remember that the social and historical context in which they lived was drastically different from ours, and their efforts and accomplishments should be considered in relation to the realities they faced. The lives discussed here are illustrative of an era of collecting, and they are worth remembering in connection to the objects they helped bring into public view.

I. Behind the Dry Ice Curtain

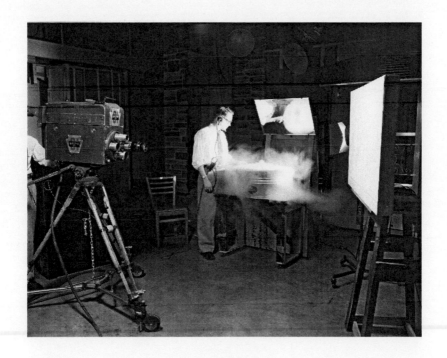

FROELICH RAINEY, a dashing man in his early forties with dark hair and square jaw, is visibly nervous, sitting on a desklike podium with a globe to his left. To his right is a small stage with three chairs in which three scholarly looking men are sitting. Overhead, white Styrofoam balls hang from the ceiling; lit from the bottom, they have the appearance of a crude solar system. The lights darken. A large, gray, tanklike television camera is before him, and the cameraman zooms in on Rainey's face. A voice comes from the cabin: "Ready, action." A red light goes on in the studio, an "On Air" sign lights up, and Rainey announces, "Welcome to *What in the World?*"

It is a Tuesday night in April 1950. Rainey has recently become director of one of Philadelphia's most renowned institutions—the University of Pennsylvania Museum of Archaeology and Anthropology. The museum is only fifty years old, but it is considered to have one of the most important collections of archeological artifacts in the world. As director, Rainey follows the many charismatic figures who brought that collection together. It is time to prove himself, to bring the museum into the modern age.

Froelich Gladstone Rainey was born in River Falls, Wisconsin, in 1907, and raised on a cattle ranch in Montana. He first thought he would be a cowboy but soon developed an interest in writing. Rainey had a distinguished academic career, obtaining a bachelor's degree from the University of Chicago and doctorates in English from the American School in France and anthropology from Yale, where he studied West Indian archaeology. But, as he himself wrote, he soon wanted to go beyond the world of books: "I was . . . itching to be away from the depressing atmosphere of my third university and the deadly Midwestern pursuit for culture. Born and bred in the western United States, I longed to discover for myself another and older world."[2] The nation's economy was crashing in 1929 as Rainey boarded a commercial steamer in San Francisco. In his travels he had many interesting experiences: selling ten-gallon tins of kerosene along roadsides in the Philippines, spending a night in a Cairo jail for carrying a gun, being stranded penniless in Shanghai, and supporting himself for a while as a gambler in Monte Carlo. He worked at the Yale Peabody Museum as assistant curator between 1931 and 1935. In addition, the hyperactive Rainey became the first professor of anthropology at the University of Alaska, teaching there between 1935 and 1942.

In 1944 Rainey joined the American Foreign Service and was assigned to the staff of the planned Allied Control Commission for Occupied Germany under Robert Daniel Murphy. He survived a brutal winter crossing of the North Atlantic, during which his convoy was savaged by storms and U-boat attacks, only to arrive in London as the first V-2 rocket bombs fell. After the war, Rainey continued his relationship with the United States government, traveling to Washington to work on the establishment of a branch of what would become the Central Intelligence Agency. But he wanted to return to academia.

In 1947 the opportunity of leading a museum in Philadelphia presented itself. The University Museum had

---

2. Froelich G. Rainey, *Reflections of a Digger: Fifty Years of World Archaeology* (Philadelphia: University of Pennsylvania Press), p. 1.

experienced a hiatus during the war, and with many vacant positions, an operating deficit, and an interim director, it desperately needed new energy and vision. Rainey, then forty years old, was recommended from various sides. He had an impressive resume: on top of his international experience, he had the academic credentials. The museum's board of trustees selected him enthusiastically.

Rainey remained director for almost thirty years, until 1976, a pivotal period for the institution. Over the years, he introduced new technologies for dating artifacts (some of which, including thermoluminescence dating, later came under attack; see chapter 6), new exhibition techniques, and even a "Brazilian coffee room" (a cafeteria) at the museum. Percy Madeira, who was president of the board when Rainey was hired, wrote in 1964, "Rainey seldom lets his imagination be inhibited by the practical difficulties inherent in a new idea," adding later, "Consequently, the Museum of today is very different from that of 1947."[3]

Rainey was a populist—"I have never been a dedicated scholar and disliked the label 'intellectual,'"[4] he wrote—and he was part of the first postwar generation of museum directors, which shared the belief that the education of the public is the civic role of the American museum. This democratized vision, plus an explosion of market-driven mass media, necessitated a change in the tone of museum scholarship.

In 1948 the director of education of the University Museum, Eleanor Moore, had the idea to produce educational programs about the museum for television. She

---

3. Percy C. Madeira, Jr., *Men in Search of Man* (Philadelphia: University of Pennsylvania Press, 1964), p. 56.
4. Rainey, *Reflections*, p. 28.

asked Rainey to participate in one of the programs along with Helge Larsen, a Danish anthropologist. Given a script that both thought was too stiff to follow, on the evening of the show, they decided to improvise:

> In the studio, as "visuals", were a number of objects made by Eskimos. As we went along ad-libbing our conversation it occurred to me to pick up one of the objects and as a "straight" man ask Helge what it was. Soon I began to notice that the young men in the crew on the studio floor were missing their cues. Afterward I learned that it was not only the odd things that Helge said about such strange objects, but the original, extemporaneous, and unexpected conversation. The director, with no script, was furious, but the crew loved it.
>
> Strange things by strange people in strange places obviously have some kind of appeal to those who live in the mechanical, mass-produced, regimented world of the twentieth century, and the unexpected must be a boon to those who live in a planned society. Anyway, I saw the possibility of taking archaeology and anthropology to the millions via television. Perhaps out of that would grow a satisfactory answer to that simple question: why archaeology?[5]

Rainey had witnessed the emergence of television in his youth, and he understood its language. After that epiphanic evening, he thought: Why not invest in a TV program with good production values and bring the venerable collection

---

5. Ibid., pp. 274–75.

of the University Museum into people's homes? No one before had exploited the visual capacity of television to describe and introduce museum objects. With a team of producers Rainey conceived of a loosely organized game show that would bring a panel of archaeology experts and other noted personalities together to examine a variety of ancient objects and determine their origins and the characteristics of the cultures that created them. Rainey would moderate the series. One can only imagine how such an idea must have been met by the conservative wing of the museum—the older, set-in-their-ways curators and keepers of the various collections. But Rainey was relentless, and in 1950 the first series of programs was created.

An off-stage voice, which the panelists couldn't hear but the audience could, introduced each one of the objects as it emerged on the screen through a curtain of dry ice fog, accompanied by mysterious, exotic flute music. The panelists included celebrities and artists, along with curators of the University Museum (who weren't necessarily at an advantage, as items were chosen from very diverse cultures and from obscure areas of the museum's holdings). Viewers watched as they (usually) failed to pinpoint the exact period or culture to which the object belonged. Guests' willingness to risk embarrassment speaks highly of their bravery and of Rainey's persuasive powers.

The program was a huge success. In 1951 *What in the World?* won a Peabody Award, the most coveted prize in television, for its "superb blending of the academic and the entertaining."[6] Soon the program was broadcast to

6. George Dessart, "*What in the World*: A Television Institution," *Expedition* 4, no. 1 (Fall 1961): 37.

Carleton Coon, Jacques Lipchitz, and Alfred Kidder II,
study an object, while Froelich Rainey moderates
What in the World? WCAU TV Studios, c. 1960.

eighty-nine stations in the CBS network. *Life* magazine
published a story on *What in the World?*, and the BBC soon
created a show based on the same format, titled *Animal
Vegetable and Mineral.* "Thanks to the television" Rainey
wrote, "Archaeology moved into mass media."[7]

Rainey received lots of fan mail, much of which is in
the archives of the University Museum. It appears that,
remarkably, he personally answered every letter. "We are
happy to know that you enjoy the program as much as we
have fun making it," he often wrote in his responses. *What
in the World?* continued to be popular, cycling on and off

7. Rainey, *Reflections*, p. 276.

the air for almost two decades. Eventually, though, its basic production values were eclipsed by big-budget shows, and the series was brought to a close. Yet Rainey and the museum were remembered for the program for decades, and the museum continued to convene *What in the World?* revivals every now and then, as part of benefits or special events, until 1975.

* * *

Sixty or so years after the first broadcast of *What in the World?*, it is a hot summer in Philadelphia, in 2009. I cross a plaza full of hoagie and falafel carts at Thirty-fourth and Spruce Streets and arrive for the first time at the University Museum. I am here to develop an art project for the museum, and the goal of this visit is to find some direction for my research.

Through a large gate are an open courtyard with a fountain and an agreeable group of trees. The architecture recalls the generation of Washington Irving and Frederic Church's Olanna—a fantasy combining a Moorish garden, a Romanesque church, and an Italian palazzo. The architect was Wilson Eyre, Jr., who had taken a northern Italian Renaissance style as a departure point but had internationalized it, in keeping with much of the Victorian architecture of the time. The original project was incredibly ambitious—a group of buildings set in a nine-acre landscape—but construction stopped after thirty years, during the Great Depression. The engraving on the stone slab at the main entrance reads, "Free Museum of Science and Art," the original name of the museum, between gatepost figures by Alexander Stirling Calder, the father of the famous twentieth-century American artist.

I walk through the museum's Kress entrance, part of a modern expansion in 1971. Styled like many other museum spaces of the 1970s, the space is flanked by two giant totem poles. A remarkably well-postured man with earrings and a silver bracelet welcomes me courteously. He is Bill Wierzbowski, the associate keeper of the American collection. Bill takes me through the museum for the first time. We go up and down stairs and up again, opening and closing doors. The museum is a maze of corridors, and some hallways are partially lit. There are a number of closed galleries and a few exhibits in the middle of repair. We pass sphinxes, Babylonian artifacts, African costumes, Greek vases. There is no air conditioning in most of the galleries, and surrounded by the dimly lit Mayan stelae and other artifacts in the midsummer heat, I feel as if I am in a tomb.

As in most archaeology museums, some of the cases appear to have been unaltered since the 1960s. Their light greens and blues, the fonts in which the texts are set, and the style of the mountings are all reminiscent of another era of museology. The cases are time capsules, not of the cultures they ostensibly contain and depict but of the curatorial vision of those cultures at the time they were designed. In that sense, the museum is a dual encyclopedia, of both the cultures it studies and how those cultures were perceived by our curatorial ancestors. In modern and contemporary art museums, that phenomenon is almost impossible to find: it would be like walking into the Solomon R. Guggenheim Museum to find galleries

as they were originally installed by Hilla Rebay, or finding galleries at the Museum of Modern Art that remain
untouched since the times of Alfred H. Barr, Jr.

We walk into the archives, where Alex Pezzati, the
museum's archivist for twenty years, is waiting. The
archive room of the University Museum has the feel of a
grand nineteenth-century university library. Two levels of
dark oak shelves contain hundreds of gray archival boxes
documenting the more than three hundred expeditions
that have been financed by the museum and containing the papers of many generations of museum workers.
Alex's desk sits on top of a platform at the end of the
room, supporting an old computer and piles of files. I
have been told that Alex, who despite his youthful looks
fulfills the role of institutional memory for the museum,

bears insider knowledge of the near infinitude of stories hidden in the archives as well as the oral history that has been transmitted by generations of museum staff, many of whom are deceased.

I tell him that I am interested in the lives of unusual people who have passed through the museum. "Oh, we have plenty of characters, *that* we definitely do," he says, pointing at some of the portrait paintings on the walls of the large room. I don't transcribe his remarks, but they go something like this:

That one over there is Sarah Yorke Stevenson, who became director. She really was a remarkable woman, a liberated woman from the Victorian era. She was, like, the first woman museum director ever. Well, I am not sure if *ever*, but she was considered the first in everything. I think she created the first museum studies program. That one over there was the provost who created the museum, William Pepper; they say he had an affair with Stevenson. That one over there is Maxwell Sommerville—he definitely was a character. He would dress as a Buddhist to give tours, and then he collected engraved gems, a kind that no one was interested in, and created a whole department for it. Then there was Louis Shotridge, the Alaskan Indian, who became a curator here. He died under mysterious circumstances; they say there was foul play. And of course Hermann Hilprecht, the curator of Assyriology, who got into a famous fight with John Peters over the first expedition of the museum to Nippur. He was well connected, and when he got into a fight with the museum he left with the keys to the collection and took a bunch of stuff with him. There was Byron Gordon; they say his personality was as sharp as his moustache.

Alex goes through the stories quickly, and they are so complex and intertwined that it is hard for me to get a handle on any of them. I leave the museum extremely stimulated but also intimidated.

I spend that night with Helen Cunningham and Ted Newbold, two Philadelphia philanthropists who have been involved with arts and culture in the city for many decades. When, during dinner, I mention my museum visit to Ted, he says, unprompted, "Oh yes, the University Museum. They used to have a TV program called *What in the World?* It was so fun to watch. Sometimes they would have competitions where the viewers could phone in the answer, and once I called in and won! But later they only had real archaeologists competing, and it was no fun anymore. Anyway, I don't know why they ended it. Those were good years."

* * *

The *New York Times* dismissed *What in the World?* as promoting a "stamp collector" mentality—equating knowledge with the ability to identify a given artifact.[8] But

---

8. Quoted in Ibid., p. 39.

others defended Rainey's project, saying that education has to start somewhere, and if the show reaches an audience that would have never been reached otherwise, then it has a value.[9]

The range of reactions about the show then is reminiscent of today's ongoing debate in museum education concerning "edutainment"—whether entertainment is a useful vehicle for an educational experience, or if attempts to entertain obscure or obliterate educational value. The answer, I think, depends on an institution's audience goals and what one means by "entertainment." Although some may be entertained by reading Shakespeare or Cervantes, certainly also educational experiences, the most common idea of entertainment involves a relaxation of mental expenditure, adopting a vegetative state in front of a TV screen, for example. Pairing this mode of entertainment with educational efforts seems to presuppose that knowledge can be obtained with no effort, a proposition that, to most of us, is equivalent to recommending diet pills for weight loss without exercising: intellectual growth is rarely a purely leisurely process. But this doesn't mean, conversely, that learning should be a dry and clinical process. Today, the term "engagement" is more favored in museums. It describes the alert state of mind of someone who actively interacts with an enticing as well as intellectually stimulating reality.

What in the World? introduced American audiences to archaeology and to the main cultures of the world and even inspired some to study it formally. In the surviving episodes, the simple but clever process through which Rainey involved

9. Ibid., p. 39.

his audience is evident. It functioned like a detective game in which the solution to the mystery was the true story of the object. His strategy educated viewers using two main principles of archaeology and museums: first, that we often come to artifacts in darkness, with no knowledge of them; and second, that objects carry narratives.

* * *

In my subsequent visits to the museum's archives, I continued thinking about Rainey and his program, about his quest to open the door of ancient civilizations using a group of mysterious objects. Sitting in the middle of that large room I thought that some of those artifacts, put on a pedestal for examination, could also tell the stories of those larger-than-life individuals, like Rainey, who had given life and purpose to the institution. And today, we who are not archaeology specialists (like those TV viewers) may yet be able to recognize the humanity in them; each object emerging from behind the curtain of smoke, revealing the visions of those who are gone, those whose portraits hang on the walls of the museum but whose life stories lie underground, like the objects they once uncovered. As a kid in Mexico, one of the first books I knew that addressed ancient cultures was Anita Brenner's *Idols Behind Altars* (1929). In the University Museum I saw curators behind altars—curatorial biographies waiting to reemerge from within the collections of artifacts curators once assembled, waiting for the chance to speak again.

II. Maxwell Sommerville,
Glyptologist

THE "TRIUMPH OF CONSTANTINE" IN THE SOMMERVILLE COLLECTION

"Take the veil which I hold," said the hermit, in a
    melancholy tone,
"and blind mine eyes; for I may not look on the treasure
    which thou art
presently to behold without sin and presumption."

—Sir Walter Scott, *The Talisman*, 1825

IN THE CORNER of the archives room at the University
Museum, toward the top of a circular staircase, there is a
portrait of Maxwell Sommerville, explorer, collector, and
distinguished academic. He stands in a classical pose, not
with the serious demeanor of a historical figure but with a
slight smirk, perhaps an illusory expression created by the
contour of his moustache and beard. He is depicted in the
year 1893 next to his life's work: a collection of talismans
and engraved gems including at bottom left a giant stone
known as The Triumph of Constantine. The professor
looks out of the picture, proudly displaying his jewels, as
if promising to unveil the secrets of glyptology, a field of
knowledge that he himself created.

By all accounts an imposing figure, he is usually remembered as tall and thin, with an authoritative-looking beard,
a stately demeanor, and the pose of a born performer. (Other
surviving pictures, photographs, provide a less conventional
view: in the most famous of them he is dressed as a Buddhist
priest, ready to conduct a tour of his collection of Buddhist
objects or make a religious invocation. Another, stranger
photograph depicts him bare chested, arms crossed over a

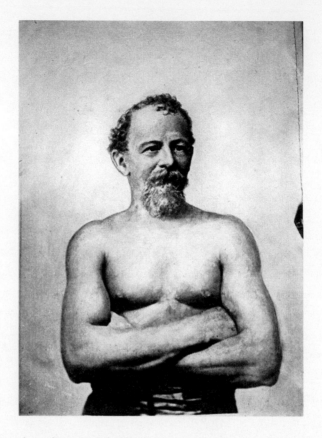

muscular physique, but it is apparent that a younger body has been pasted below an older face, paper-doll style.) A few years after the painting was made, Sommerville became the first (and likely the last) person to bear the title Professor and Curator of Glyptology at the University Museum, the institution to which he bequeathed his vast collection of gems.

Despite his prominence during his lifetime, a good deal about Sommerville's life has been lost to obscurity. We know that he was born in 1829 in Clarksburg, now West Virginia. He graduated from Central High School in Philadelphia, from which many prominent Philadelphians

have emerged. That was the extent of his formal education. He married twice, in 1863 and 1891. During the Civil War he worked at the Sherman and Company printing house in Philadelphia, through which effort he amassed a considerable amount of wealth. This in turn funded thirty years of world travel. We don't know much about those travel years, but it is certain that in that period he embraced the study of engraved gems and talismans in a unique and obsessive way. It is often mentioned that he inherited this interest from his grandfather, James McAlpin, who was a collector. McAlpin was a Freemason, and he introduced young Max to the principles of the practice. Sommerville entered Union Lodge in Philadelphia on February 9, 1865, and obtained memberships in many other chapters. The hermetic evocations of Masonic symbolism resonate with his intense fascination with the mystery of the foreign talismans he collected.

The best way to get a sense of Sommerville's voice and his passion for his field is to read his 1889 book, *Engraved Gems: Their History and an Elaborate View of Their Place in Art.* Sommerville's view is indeed elaborate; he expounds it over 783 pages that are less a scientific study of his collection or of cultural periods than a compilation of personal recollections from the many trips he took to acquire the objects. Sommerville's research was little more than traveling around purchasing items, but it is clear how strongly he felt that engraved gems were important microcosms of history and culture. At the beginning of the book he describes what will follow in its pages:

> We will walk upon the crumbled ruins of bygone centuries, our retrospective view shall be where changing elements, rust, and age have spared but traces of palaces and temples; we will stroll beside a rapid stream until we reach a grove where I have oft turned in and found a rich repast; no shrines, no obelisks, no statues, naught but these precious little stepping stones, by which we will cross the stream, and in the vale of antiquity with these miniature monuments, study and enjoy the indelible portraiture of the ages.[10]

10. Maxwell Sommerville, *Engraved Gems: Their History and an Elaborate View of Their Place in Art* (Philadelphia: Sherman and Co., 1889), p. 8.

The book includes one hundred elegant engravings based on drawings by Sommerville, which, evidencing some graphic talent, vary from close depictions of collectibles to incongruous illustrations of the author walking into his favorite shop in Paris or purchasing a pair of Greek shoes. For him, life experience and research were inextricable from each other.

In 1889, when the book was published, Sommerville's collection was already on view at the Metropolitan Museum of Art, New York, where it remained until 1891. The director of the museum at the time, Luigi di Cesnola, was impressed with Sommerville's gems and hoped at some point to obtain them for the Met. This kind of recognition must have been a source of great pride and a sense of vindication for this man with only a high school education, a lack of credentials that likely made him feel insecure next to more accomplished archaeologists and explorers. Although his rise had been unorthodox and outside the usual channels in his field, Sommerville had found a scholarly niche for himself in the upper strata of American academia through experience facilitated by his great wealth.

In 1894, five years after the publication of *Engraved Gems*, Sommerville was made Professor of Glyptology at the University of Pennsylvania. But what was glyptology? Around the time of his appointment, Sommerville had coined a name for his field—the study of precious engraved gems (in which he was nearly the only practitioner)—and then lobbied to make it an accepted field in academia. According to Sommerville's nemesis, the eminent curator Stewart Culin, who was the first director of the University

Museum and worked with the professor from 1892 to 1903 (he went on to become a well-known ethnographer and curator at the Brooklyn Museum), there had been a bit of an academic conspiracy: "It was said through the intervention of the President of the Corporation with the Editors of the Dictionary that the word glyptology was added officially to our language," around the time of Sommerville's appointment.[11]

At some point in his career, Sommerville developed a fascination with Buddhism, and this became a second specialty. He devoted a good deal of his travels to the gathering of Buddhist materials, and in the late 1890s he began lobbying the university to import an entire Buddhist temple to Philadelphia. After some back and forth, it was decided that a temple would be installed in the new University Museum, founded just a decade before. Culin wrote that once the various crates containing the temple began arriving at the museum, in 1898, Sommerville "closed [the gallery] from the public eye and as far as I can recall held no public communication with me except to ask me if I could recommend him to a thoroughly reliable Chinese laundryman."[12] He spent nearly a year in the gallery, working in complete secrecy. Finally, in spring 1899, he sent out elaborate invitations to the opening of the temple.

May 3, 1899, was, perhaps, the most important day of Maxwell Sommerville's life—the great culmination of a lifetime of travels and scholarship. On that day a

---

11. Stewart Culin "The Professor of Glyptology" (Culin Archival Collection, Brooklyn Museum, New York), p. 6.
12. Ibid., p. 8.

"WITHIN THE CHANCEL RAIL"

small group of reporters gathered to get a glimpse of the first Buddhist temple ever assembled inside a museum. According to the reports, six tons of material had been shipped from Japan, and Sommerville emphasized that every single piece of material in the gallery had come from the East. He explained to the press that the temple was not "Korean, Tibetan, Chinese or Japanese, nor of any other Oriental nation" but rather made "from materials purchased of priests in charge of Buddhist temples of many eastern lands."[13] Judging from photographs, the installation was an improvised shrine containing hundreds of objects of every kind, including divinities in bronze, bells, drums, lanterns, paintings, and other ornaments, in wood or fabric. Two large statues—the *Zuijin*, or temple guardians—flanked the entrance. The various Buddhas, the image of a sacred

13. Sommerville, Monograph of the Buddhist Temple in the Free Museum of Science and Art (Philadelphia, 1904), p. 3.

white elephant, and innumerable other objects relating to different modes of worship seem to have overwhelmed the reporters. The *Philadelphia Times* journalist was one of the most impressed; he describes "a scene of Oriental splendor, the glare of searchlights bringing out the glistening effect of the golden deities, the richly embroidered panels and the highly colored hangings."[14] The *Philadelphia Press* reporter was more skeptical: "To the casual observer the interior of the temple is a confusion of oriental color, gods, shrines, ritualistic paraphernalia and weird and rich embroideries. Deities of brass, wood, stone, great and small and all ugly, are scattered here, there, everywhere."[15]

Sommerville demonstrated worship activities at the temple in a brocaded Buddhist robe. In a photograph in a museum education guidebook, Sommerville can be seen in the corner of the room in his Buddhist attire. Like the dwarf who famously functioned as both a guide to and an item in Ulisse Aldrovandi's cabinet of curiosities during the Renaissance, Sommerville was an extension of his own temple. Historian Steven Conn has made a comparison with the theater: "The temple became a stage and Sommerville its leading man."[16] Sommerville certainly appeared more interested in performing for an audience than teaching one.

Culin's biographical sketch of Sommerville provides a glimpse of its subject's innate performative qualities. Culin

14. *Philadelphia Times*, May 4, 1899. University Museum Archives.
15. *Philadelphia Press* article, quoted by Elizabeth Lyons in "Maxwell Sommerville, 1829–1904" (University Museum Archives, December 1985).
16. Conn, "Going Native for an Afternoon: Maxwell Sommerville, His Buddhist Temple and the Search for a Usable Asia" (University Museum Archives, 2004).

narrates receiving a mysterious invitation to an event at Sommerville's house before he had become acquainted with him, possibly sometime in the late 1880s. When he arrived he was taken to a darkened room where guests sat facing a curtain. At some point the grave professor emerged in his Buddhist garb, speaking in tongues. After the performance the admiring audience commented enthusiastically about the experience. Later, Sommerville, surrounded by servants or helpers (which, based on Culin's descriptions and illustrations of the Buddhist temple, were of African or Asian heritage), took his guests to see his vast collection of gems and talismans. He was a man in search of an audience. In fact, he was not only the first person to install a temple inside an American museum and the first to attempt interpretive history through theater in the galleries—he was an early practitioner of what is now derisively called "edutainment," teaching through spectacle.

Sommerville's doctrinary and exoticist scholarship of the Orient is not unusual for his time, although even in the late nineteenth century his academic prose must have seemed romanticized and sentimental (it was likely inspired by the Orientalist travel writers of time, probably more the French [Gérard de Nerval, Pierre Loti] than the British). Today it is hard not to frown at his approach and at the way the press shaped the collector as a hero. Harry Dillon Jones, a writer for *The Booklovers Magazine*, described Sommerville's last African expedition thus: "With a caravan consisting of sixteen Persian horses, half a dozen camels, and twenty servants and guides, he penetrated fearlessly into the interior of the Desert of Sahara" (although with so many horses, servants and guides, what could he have had to fear?).[17] Many stories of his travels recount his adventures in obtaining an important amulet or piece of jewelry from a reluctant villager or tribe in a foreign land, with patronizing comments about the sellers, who in Sommerville's view were unable to appreciate the value of what they were selling.

Sommerville's desire to promote glyptology and Buddhism in the West contrasted with his almost exclusively pragmatic view of the peoples he visited. While unceasingly intrigued and fascinated by the objects he purchased, he didn't appear equally fond of or interested in the living cultures that had produced them. Regarding a trip to Thailand in 1897, he was quoted as dismissing all of Thai cuisine: "The diet, being peculiar to the people of the country, was not palatable to European travelers . . . a native traveler and guest would be offered a repast of more than forty dishes, of none of which any of our race would care to partake in."[18] In describing his experiences in a street in Constantinople, Sommerville complained of "the monotonous strains of rude music, the symphonies [sic] of the Arabic race, which, falling weirdly on our tutored ears, were charming in the antithesis: the very recollection of these strange tones gives us by contrast a greater appreciation of the purer and entrancing melodies peculiar to our higher civilization."[19]

Ironically, Sommerville also didn't seem to have much

17. Harry Dillon Jones, "Gods, Gems and Mascots: The Life-Work of Maxwell Sommervile" *The Booklovers Magazine* 4, no. 1 (July 1904): 64.
18. Sommerville, quoted in John Shaw, "Farang Fables", *City Life Chiang May*, Vol. 11, No. 10 (2002).
19. Sommerville, *Engraved Gems*, p. 294.

regard for the members of "our higher civilization" he was trying to educate. He organized tours of the Buddhist temple for Japanese students at the university, but the visitors he received were mainly elderly society ladies there to hear his religious invocations. Culin reports that the professor was frustrated at visitors' unwillingness to prostrate themselves at the shrine, and he responded to their naïve questions with ire. "It was this very severity, this jealousy of his position that led to the catastrophy that sundered our relations," he adds.

Due partially to his temperamental character and to his frictions with Culin and other curators, Sommerville's relationships at the museum deteriorated toward his final days. He reportedly fainted once, when he found himself excluded from a lecture series Culin had organized, and at the height of the tensions he threatened to retire his bequests.

Sommerville died in 1904. In the end, he did leave his collection to the museum. According to keeper Elizabeth Lyons it was so vast and disorganized that it took years to catalogue. She described him as "this man who inundated our storage with his vacuum cleaner, eclectic collection."[20]

In his *Booklovers Magazine* article, which was published after Sommerville's death, Harry Dillon Jones praised his life and work calling him a "public spirited mortal" and a "learned traveler, eminent archaeologist, tireless collector."[21] A newspaper article praises him as "one of the largest and most important representatives of glyptic art in America." But not everyone held him in high esteem. In 1907 John

---

20. Lyons, "Maxwell Sommerville," p.2.
21. Jones, "Gods, Gems and Mascots," p. 59.

S. Lopez, in *Appleton's Magazine*, called him a "pathetic figure of an ingenuous old gentleman with a hobby . . . the most pathetic figure that ever trod the walks of higher education."[22] Culin described him as "a man, who with all kindliness and charity I may designate as a fraud and an impostor through and through."[23]

For after Sommerville's death, the authenticity of his gems and other objects was put into question. A renowned German scholar, Dr. A. Furtwangler, who on a passing visit through Philadelphia had a chance to examine the collection, declared in 1905 in the *American Journal of Archaeology* that "the engraved gems, from the collection of Maxwell Sommerville, are chiefly forgeries."[24] This caused a small scandal in the archaeology community, but over time it became increasingly clear that much of what Sommerville had collected were indeed cheap imitations or forgeries.

A newspaper article published the day after Sommerville's glyptology collection went on display at the University Museum reports that the items had been obtained "from the credulous people only because they were in starving condition."[25] In fact it would appear that he had been taken been taken advantage of by skilled forgers—the same ones whom he had derided in his adventures—who had exploited his insatiable thirst for unique items.

But had he really been completely in the dark? When

22. John S. Lopez, "The Hoodwinking of American Collectors," *Appleton's Magazine* 9, no. 3, March (1907): 336.
23. Culin, "The Professor of Glyptology," p. 6.
24. A. Furtwangler, "Antiquities in Museums: United States," *American Journal of Archaeology* (Vol. 9, 1905) p. 366.
25. Lopez, "The Hoodwinking of American Collectors," p. 336.

we look at his other great project, the Buddhist temple, the story is slightly different. Culin had been skeptical about the temple, but it must have been difficult for him to publicly criticize the project at the time from his position as a museum representative. He recognized, for example, that several red paper labels featured "hieroglyphics" written by the Chinese laundryman that he himself had recommended to the professor.[26] Later Sommerville had confided to Culin that he had built most of the architectural fragments himself, using wood from the crates that had held the objects—so he could say truly that all the items in the room had come from the East.

According to Lopez's article in *Appleton's Magazine,* a visit to the temple by a Japanese delegation "led to the discovery, it is said, that the wondrous temple collection was a jumble of inconsistencies, largely filled with spurious objects. It was even charged that some of these supposed ancient prayer rolls were in fact modern Japanese advertising posters."[27]

Given Sommerville's conscious attempts to fake the authenticity of his temple, one naturally wonders about the extent to which he may have consciously hid the fact that many of his gems were not the ancient objects he claimed they were. The earnestness and conviction of his writings, nonetheless, his theatrical displays, and the drama that he instilled in his narratives are not those of a forger but of a man living under a gentle delusion. He probably wanted so much to believe in their authenticity that for him there were no doubts about their origin.

---

26. Culin, "The Professor of Glyptology," p. 9.
27. Lopez, "The Hoodwinking of American Collectors," p. 340.

The Triumph of Constantine, the prized stone depicted in Sommerville's portrait, was also alleged to be a fake. Sommerville had provided a detailed provenance for it:

> Amongst the most important and interesting antique gems in my collection is one engraved when Constantine held the Roman Empire in Bizantia, which came into the possession of the Court of Russia. The Empress Catherine II, wishing to confer a great favor and special regard on an ambassador to her court, from her remarkable collection in the Museum of the Hermitage at St. Petersburg, presented this antique gem to him in 1785. Twenty-five years afterwards, at his death in Greece, it was sold, and was piously guarded during thirty years by a collector in the Hellenic peninsula. After that it became the property of Bieler in Styria. I came into possession of this remarkable gem after more than five years of negotiations with its owner, and subsequently with his heirs.[28]

About this, Lopez, the *Appleton's* writer, wrote, "It is now alleged that Professor Sommerville's 'Triumph of Constantine' was fabricated in a small shop in Germany, said to be devoted to the manufacture of bogus antiquities, and that clever agents of the establishment brought it to the attention of the victim, and then, stipulating secrecy, successfully negotiated its sale . . . The genuine 'Triumph of Constantine' reposes in the Imperial Museum of Vienna."[29]

In an attempt corroborate this account, I contacted the

28. Sommerville, quoted in Ibid.
29. Ibid., p. 340.

Kunsthistorisches Museum in Vienna (formerly the Imperial Museum). Via e-mail, Dr. Afred Berhard-Walcher, director of the museum's antiquities collection, wrote that the piece is indeed in its collection (cat. IXa–69) but added, "Material/ medium is chalcedony [a mineral from the Chalcedon region of Asia Minor], measures 5.3 × 8.5 cm. It has been in the art trade since 1869. Our cameo is like the cameo in Philadelphia (from the Sommerville collection, earlier the Biehler collection, Vienna) and numerous other cameos—a modern fabrication/fake, which traces back to depictions of the Arch of Titus (from the old views of the 18th century). Already in 1899, this cameo was described in the technical literature as modern (E. Peterson, *Moderne Kaiserkameen* [Modern Emperor Cameos], *Römische Mitteilungen* [Roman Studies], XIV, 1899, 244–250)."

Although the Vienna and Philadelphia cameos are dissimilar in many ways—their materials and aspects of their imagery differ—they both clearly are interpretations of one of the reliefs of the Arch of Titus in Rome. Sommerville had purchased not even an expert reproduction of an original cameo, but one of several eighteenth-century fakes designed after a famous relief depicting Titus, not Constantine, one of which was acknowledged to be modern during the collector's lifetime. Despite all this, the cameo continued to make appearances at the University Museum. It was used as the cover illustration of a 1956 catalogue for an exhibition show organized by Cornelius C. Vermeule. Today, acknowledged as Neoclassical, it is on display in a corner of the museum.

Pioneering any field—even one self-created—is a remarkable endeavor, and the pioneer inevitably navigates an uncharted road, making all sorts of mistakes. For all his gullibility and naïve idealism, for all his desire to ascend to the academic heights of collecting and curatorship, Sommerville was an Orientalist of his time who fervently believed that Eastern objects must be preserved and studied, and he used his wealth to that end and as much intellect as he had been allotted. Not everything he collected was fake, and regardless of its authenticity his collection is a valuable portrait of an era in academia, museology, and the study of antiquities. Sommerville's legacy also includes the first "immersive" environment in a museum (the Buddhist temple), his generosity, his desire to communicate his enthusiasm for other times and cultures, and that innate performative drive that would have made him an inspired installation or performance artist today.

Sommerville left $30,000 to the museum in addition to his collection. Beyond that, his will was full of intriguing bequests: he left money to the Masonic temple and the home for training in speech for deaf children in Philadelphia, two clerks in his favorite Paris hotel, the Union Syndicale des Contrôleurs de la Compagnie Generale des Omnibus de Paris (the Parisian bus-drivers' union), and a certain Parisian Madame, known as Petite Marie, chief of a lingerie department (perhaps the woman for whom the athletic photographic pastiche was made). Now, a darkening historical figure, he is like one of his beloved talismans, elusive in origin, self constructing his own mythology.

III. Love and Madness in Nippur

IN ALMOST EVERY history of the origins of the University Museum there is a reproduction of a photograph taken around 1899 by John Henry Haynes during the museum's archaeological expedition to Nippur, one of the most ancient of Sumerian cities, in what is now Iraq. The striking albumen print displays, in high contrast, the semiburied ruins of the ziggurat of Enlil, the main god of the Mesopotamian pantheon. The picture, taken from the top of the ziggurat, is a bird's-eye view of the scene. The starkly beautiful picture recalls the compositions of the Hudson River School and the Romantic landscapes of Caspar David Friedrich, in a seeming fulfillment of the Orientalist fantasies of the nineteenth century. The dark shadows suggest that it is evening. Around fifty people, anonymous silhouettes, walk to or from an extended mound near the structure, which shines bright on the horizon, giving the scene a kind of aura of light. The vast empty landscape is nonetheless slightly unsettling: it underscores the figures' smallness in the massive desolation of the desert.

Throughout its history, the University Museum has sponsored hundreds of archaeological expeditions around the world. Of them, the very first one, the Nippur expedition, which unfolded episodically in four campaigns between 1889 and 1900, is the most legendary. Its story is charged with drama, combining success and failure, tragedy and scholarly achievement, and a historic academic wrestling match that pitted two of the expedition's dominating figures against each other, a drama that is still recalled with smiles by archaeologists.

The protagonists were the self-proclaimed hero of the expedition—the legendary German Assyriologist and University of Pennsylvania professor Hermann Vollrath Hilprecht—and Episcopal-minister-turned-archaeologist-turned-minister John P. Peters, who raised funds for the initial trip and was on-site during the first and second campaigns.

The relationship between Hilprecht and Peters had never been a good one. They had personal tensions from the very first campaign, when Peters supposedly laughed at Hilprecht when he fell from his horse during the ride to Nippur.[30] The legendary Hilprecht-Peters controversy began in 1905, five years after the expedition ended, when Peters accused Hilprecht of publishing an inaccurate

---

30. William H. Witte, interview by J. A. Mason (University Museum Archives, July 26, 1953) p. 4.

account of the four Nippur campaigns.[31] Hilprecht had published a massive, six-hundred-page volume in 1903 entitled *Explorations in Bible Lands*, with contributions from various scholars, detailing accounts of expeditions to various regions of the Middle East. The book dedicated around 450 pages to Nippur with an emphasis on Hilprecht's role. This account unnerved the international

31. For the most accurate and complete description of the controversy and of the Nippur expedition, see Bruce Kuklick, *Puritans in Babylon: The Ancient Near East and American Intellectual Life, 1880–1930* (Princeton, N.J.: Princeton University Press, 1996).

Assyriology community and particularly the American academics, among whom the foreign Hilprecht was already unpopular. In private correspondence among them, Hilprecht was described as "a bag of wind," and a "humbug," and his "egotism" and "desire for cheap notoriety" were "well-nigh miraculous."[32]

According to Peters, Hilprecht had intentionally misrepresented his own role, claiming all the successes, and distorted the nature of the findings at Nippur—for example, Peters argued that some of the cuneiform tablets that Hilprecht had published in his book had not come from Nippur but instead had been purchased in the antiquities market. Hilprecht, who was well connected in Philadelphia society, had an acute sense of politics and the superior scholarly credentials, and he made every effort to prove his ownership of the expedition and the veracity of his historical attributions of the artifacts recovered. The scandal nonetheless enveloped the international community of Assyriologists and the staff of the museum and the university, threatening at the time to consume the museum permanently.

In all the debates about what had happened in the field, one voice was absent. Hilprecht had been at the site for the first three months of the first campaign and then for a few weeks during the last campaign, in 1900, and Peters had been in the field for the first two years (during the first and second campaigns) of the ten-year expedition. In contrast to them, John Henry Haynes was the only researcher

32. Quoted in Kuklick, "My Life's Shattered Work!: The Strange Ordeal of Hermann Hilprecht," *Odyssey* (May/June 2000): 35.

who had been present throughout all four campaigns. He had conducted most of the excavations, obtained the vast majority of the artifacts, created over two thousand glass plate negatives, and submitted thousands of typewritten reports documenting the site. He, of all people, was the most qualified to speak authoritatively about what had happened in Nippur and was, perhaps, the most entitled to receive credit for it. However, he had paid the highest personal price in the process of completing his job: by 1905, after more than a decade of exposure to the punishing conditions of desert excavation, Haynes had gone insane.

John Henry Haynes was born in Rowe, Massachusetts, in 1849, and grew up there on his father's farm. His father died while he was still in school, and young John took over the many labors of the farm. Of Haynes, C.Q. Richmond, a later acquaintance, reported, "There is the tradition that he promised his mother not to leave [the farm] until the mortgage of the farm was paid. This may not be strictly true but we may at least be certain that he promised this much to himself."[33] (This anecdote reinforces the general perception that Haynes had, according to Richmond, "a passion for service, for self-sacrifice, and for duty."[34]) Haynes graduated from Williams College in 1876 with a B.A. degree. He was known there as Father Haynes, due to his sober demeanor. "His qualities were not those of brilliancy," a classmate recalled, "his mind worked slowly, yet he was patient, persevering, slow and deliberate of speech . . . he was reserved, keeping his council to him-

33. C. Q. Richmond, quoted in "The Haynes Memorial Tablet," *North Adams Evening Transcript*, Saturday, December 9, 1916, p. 3.
34. Ibid.

self . . . he was not a solitary and liked the fellowship of comrades."[35]

Despite his deliberate mien, Haynes was adventurous and wanted a life outside the confines of Massachusetts. In 1880 he left a job as principal in a high school to join an archaeological expedition to Crete. His mission was to assist William James Stillman, a famous artist and photographer with associations with the Hudson River School. Stillman was often described as "the American

35. Ibid.

Pre-Raphaelite." While the expedition was stalled in Athens, waiting for a permit to dig, Stillman taught Haynes photographic techniques. Stillman's dramatic stagecraft in field photography, best seen in his pictures of the Acropolis, was a central influence on Haynes's later depictions of the ruins in Nippur.

Haynes spent much of the 1880s in the Middle East, teaching in Constantinople and traveling. In 1884 he joined the Wolfe expedition, organized by the University of Pennsylvania to survey unexplored monuments and sites of Asia Minor. In 1888 the university invited Haynes to join its first expedition to the Middle East as business manager, photographer, and field director. It was decided that the city of Niffer (ancient Nippur) was the most promising site to explore. To facilitate the work, the Babylonian Exploration Fund (BEF, the body created at the University of Pennsylvania to fund the expedition) convinced the State Department that the United States government should create a consular position in the region. In 1889 Haynes unexpectedly received the (now perhaps dubious) honor of being the first American consul in Baghdad—although it is hard to imagine how he managed to perform any consular duties on an archaeological site in the middle of the desert, there is surviving correspondence from Haynes to the State Department providing information on various matters, such as an outbrek of cholera in the region in 1889.

The first Nippur campaign was a disaster. The ancient city had been irrigated by the Euphrates River, but the site had become a deeply inhospitable site of burning sun, dust, and insects. Additionally, the region was surrounded by hostile tribes run by local warlords who could not be effectively governed by the Ottoman government, and the Americans found themselves constantly under attack. One night, after a dispute, local tribesmen burned the whole encampment and stole the money that had been entrusted to Haynes.

Despite the chaos, the meager findings of the first campaign generated enough excitement back in Philadelphia that the university's provost, William Pepper, urged the funders to support a second campaign. Hilprecht, who had joined the first campaign but was too comfortable in academia to deal with the nastiness of the desert, refused to go back, so the second team was composed only of Peters, Haynes, and an interpreter.

It was toward the close of the second campaign that efforts started paying off. Aided by 350 hired diggers, at the end of the 1891 season the group found a number of cuneiform tablets. It was not the kind of great discovery the university had expected—it was hoped that they would find a colossal winged sculpture or an effigy of a god that could be placed in the grand atrium of the museum, to compete with the British Museum and the Louvre. Still, the discovery of the clay tablets was enough to support a third campaign.

This time it was Peters who refused to go back to the field—the hardships of the desert were too much for him, and he decided to go back to the church. Without Peters and Hilprecht, the only person left to lead the operation was Haynes. So in 1893 the third campaign was initiated, and Haynes spent the next three years in the desert, mostly by himself, digging and filing reports with the BEF and with Peters, who remained in Philadelphia as the scientific director of the expedition.

Haynes was a talented photographer, attentive to detail, dutiful, and dedicated, but he was no trained archaeologist. He did not really know how to conduct a digging, and he did not receive clear instructions from Philadelphia. Peters and Hilprecht had a rather low regard for Haynes's intellectual ability and constantly complained about his slowness and the lack of method in his work. It must have reminded him of that farm in Rowe, of trying to fill the shoes of his deceased father.

The three years Haynes spent at the site during the third campaign were likely brutal. Living most of that time in solitude, he longed for the company of others as he tried to go on with his work. His reports were some hybrid between an impersonal government report and the diary of Robinson Crusoe. About a break in the work, he wrote, "After one year of unceasing toil, under conditions which were trying alike to mind and body, the writer left the constantly changing scenes of action at Niffer for a much needed season of rest and recuperation."[36] He sometimes complained in his dispatches about being left alone at the site among the dust and insects, which, he wrote in 1894, "annoy us beyond power of description."[37]

For the most part, in his reports Haynes provided an almost infinite amount of information without saying much, giving extensive descriptions of his work but little insight into the larger scope of the investigation. Haynes

---

36. John Henry Haynes, "Nippur, Narrative of Third Campaign, Second Version" (University Museum Archives, #230, 1896).
37. Haynes, letter to Peters (University Museum Archives, 1894).

became very interested in the architecture of the site as
he started uncovering a ziggurat. He provided various
descriptions of the structures, exasperating the board of
the BEF, which could not have been less interested in
physical objects that could not be taken to Philadelphia:
they wanted artifacts.

And soon they got them. Over the course of the
expedition, Haynes dug out more than thirty thousand
cuneiform clay tablets, which he regularly shipped to
Philadelphia via Constantinople. Many of the tablets contained ancient Sumerian mythological narratives, making
the group likely the largest body of Sumerian literature
ever found and possibly the oldest texts extant (cuneiform
writing is at least as old as Egyptian hieroglyphs, and
possibly older). As the excavated tablets became more

numerous, Haynes started to refer to them in correspondence as "the 'library.' "[38]

Hilprecht was under pressure from the BEF to prove that the campaign had generated at least one major discovery. Given the absence of any colossal sculptures, Hilprecht made the best of the recent information, taking Haynes's lead and claiming that they had found the "Temple Library of Nippur." This powerful title gave the collection of tablets a status akin to the library of Alexandria and was, in retrospect, an exaggeration: today we know that Haynes had uncovered a scribal quarter, likely the private residences of scribes, where they taught and stored reference texts and the tablets on which their students wrote their lessons. Many tablets bear beginner exercises for the young scribes, who would copy lines of wedge-shaped characters as grade-school kids copy English characters today. Others bear copies of sacred texts or are legal and commercial records.

Haynes left the site for Baghdad in 1894, to take a break from a "lonely and desolate life" in "Robberdom and Murderland," he wrote. "Few people know what it is like to live alone, and no one who has ever attempted to live without companionship among brutal, scheming, thieving, and murderous tribes of feud-brewing robbers can ever know the mental tension."[39] In Baghdad Haynes met and befriended Joseph A. Meyer, an American graduate student in the Department of Architecture at the Massachusetts Institute of Technology, who was traveling

---

38. Haynes quoted in Kuklick, "My Life's Shattered Work!," pp. 31 and 34.
39. Haynes, quoted in Kuklick, *Puritans in Babylon*, p. 67.

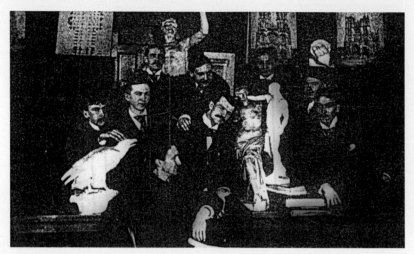

Joseph A. Meyer, Jr., (seated) with fellow students in the Architecture Library of the Massachusetts Institute of Technology, ca. 1887–91.

around the region. Haynes invited Meyer to join him at the dig and Meyer accepted. His presence at the site had a positive impact on the campaign and changed Haynes's mood, which improved his reporting to Philadelphia and gave him new energy. Meyer's architectural background reinforced Haynes's interest in the architecture of the site. They both did a lot of tracing of the ancient city, and Meyer developed many accurate and useful drawings. Haynes was exhilarated to have a companion in his ordeal. In the isolation of the desert, Meyer and Haynes developed a powerful platonic bond that seemed to go beyond the usual friendship.

Haynes's happiness did not last long, as toward September of that year Meyer became ill, probably with dysentery. Haynes's reports declined in quality again. In Philadelphia, Peters displayed very little compassion, only demanding from Haynes more results and more accurate reporting. Peter's harshness troubled William Pepper, now the ex-provost, who became concerned about Haynes's mental health.

Meyer continued to decline. He was sent to Baghdad for medical care but died shortly before Christmas that year, and Haynes was alone once again. In subsequent reports he sounded deeply in pain, and it was clear to everyone at the university that he was on the verge of a nervous breakdown. Even Hilprecht, who was not known to have been sympathetic to anyone, was concerned about Haynes and started speaking highly of the work he was doing in Nippur. However, the fact that Peters was so critical of Haynes must have been an incentive to take his side.

Two British assistants were dispatched to the site, but floods and other complications in their travel prevented them from reaching it. Haynes's letters were almost paranoid; he wrote that the situation, with violence and constant harassment from the local tribes, had become untenable. This was the end of the third campaign. As a result of the tensions in the field and in Philadelphia, in 1895 the BEF took the scientific directorship away from Peters and gave it to Haynes, ensuring him a year of respite to regroup and recover physically and mentally from his exertions.

The fourth and last campaign was organized and launched in 1899. Pepper had passed away, and the new provost, Charles Harrison, provided the funding, with the help of two wealthy supporters, Edward and Clarence Clark—brothers from an influential banking family. This time around Haynes was sent as director along with two assistants, Valentine Geere, who had a bit of experience in the field, and Clarence C. Fischer, a young recent graduate from the university. And, to the astonishment of the overseers of the project at the university, Haynes asked permission to bring his wife, Cassandria, along to Nippur. This most unusual request indicated trouble ahead to all concerned except Haynes, as archaeology, like many disciplines, was a boy's club, and bringing a woman into such a challenging environment was considered madness. But given the history of Haynes's isolation in the field, the BEF had no choice but to accede.

The atmosphere of the camp during the fourth campaign was very different in tone from the third. Cassandria Haynes introduced a kind of civility into the living conditions that had been completely absent before. However, there were also some peculiar dramas, such as the bickering of the Hayneses and tension between Geere and Cassandria, who was protective of her husband and became his assistant in writing notes and reports. At the same time, Fischer, who was an impressionable and shy young man, fell in love with Geere. Geere did not reciprocate but apparently didn't do much to fend him off, and Fischer became almost suicidal.[40]

Despite the continuing discovery of tablets, the campaign team was gradually turning into a dysfunctional family, hurling accusations at one another. Geere, in particular, was annoyed by Haynes, whom he considered irritatingly incompetent and incapable of leading the excavations in a professional manner. The BEF, becoming

40. Kuklick, *Puritans in Babylon*, p. 89.

concerned, pressured Hilprecht to go to Nippur. After some resistance he returned to the field on March 1900, after eleven years of absence, and stayed until the campaign concluded, ten weeks later.

Hilprecht immediately realized the extent of the site's mismanagement: Haynes had worked to the best of his knowledge but had not conducted digging in a professional manner. Hilprecht took command of the operation, and although he was not a professional digger himself, helped push things along using new statigraphic techniques. With his usual modesty, Hilprecht described himself in his final reports to the BEF as the savior of the campaign— although, in fact, the vast majority of the clay tablets had already been unearthed by Haynes before his arrival. Still, the university was impressed with Hilprecht and gave him a hero's welcome upon his return to Philadelphia shortly after the end of the expedition in May 1900. It is easy to imagine him speaking eloquently, to the awe of high society, about the tribulations and crises that *he* had faced in the desert and giving dramatic interviews to the press about the important discoveries he had made. Hilprecht may have not done much in the field, but his dramatic visit at the end of the campaign gave him the edge, at least at the time, to win the political struggle for owner-ship of the Nippur expedition. Even despite the fact that he eventually fell from grace with the university and the archaeology community—after which he retired to his home in Jena, Germany, taking a lot of the Babylonian tablets with him—his name still looms large in the history of the Nippur expedition and in the first chapters of the history of the search for ancient Mesopotamia.

At the end of the fourth campaign, Haynes was in poor health, with continuous fevers. He was absent from celebrations of the campaign's return, as if he had been relegated to his old job as assistant or mere facilitator. He had come back without the mental or physical disposition to take ownership of his own accomplishments or at least to create his own narrative of the expedition. The BEF claimed Haynes's successes as their own and blamed him for all the shortcomings, while celebrating Hilprecht. Additionally, after their return, Cassandria left him—disappointed, perhaps, in the man that she thought would one day become a rich and famous explorer—and Haynes lost the only person who had spoken on his behalf. His health was uncertain from that time, but his insanity was not explicitly mentioned until the time of the 1905 controversy.[41]

The last place left for him was, apparently, his sister's house in North Adams. He died there on June 29, 1910. The local authorities paid him a small tribute, unveiling a plaque in his honor a few years later. On his gravestone is an engraving of the Nippur ziggurat, the place that he had so obsessively photographed and mapped despite the lack of interest from the university in his research.

According to Philip Jones, associate curator at the University Museum, "What we find now as we go back into the archives was that Haynes had recorded things reasonably well considering the times. He is a great pioneer of archaeology. He is basically a forgotten man these days, but he is the hero of this expedition."[42] Today Wikipedia

---

41. Notes on the 1905 Hilprecht-Peters controversy (University Museum Archives).
42. Philip Jones, interview with the author, December 2009.

has an entry for Hilprecht and for Peters but none for Haynes. His name has become a footnote in a story that he mainly wrote, like the student scribes in ancient Mesopotamia whose tablets he rescued by the thousands. Without knowing it, perhaps, he spent the larger portion of his life transcribing a story for others to claim authorship of. His was the anonymous hand that, at the cost of his own sanity, traced the ancient city, dug out its texts, and pushed the shutter that captured the light and flying dust of that forsaken place in history.

IV. Louis Shotridge and the Ghost of Courageous Adventurer

In the University Museum's collection there is an enigmatic object that would have been a perfect selection for Froelich Rainey's television program. The item, known as Ghost of Courageous Adventurer, is a knife with an iron blade and guard. The texture at the edge of the blade suggests rough manufacture and old age, and the handle is wrapped with wild goat's hair and has at its blunt end a skull of ivory and abalone shell. The skull, represented with only the top mandible, looks ominously at the user. The knife is an *at.óow*, made by a member of the Tlingit people, indigenous inhabitants of the Pacific Northwest. *At.óow* means "purchased object" in Tlingit, but they are ancestral items, conveying and reminding the group of its history and identity.

In the March 1920 issue of the *Museum Journal* there is an article about the piece, explaining its provenance:

> I obtained this old knife from the last of Thunder Bird House group of the *Shungu-kaydi* clan of the Chilkat. It was the only object that carried with it to the present day a record of the important part that the clan took in establishing a trade connection between the northern Tlingit and the alien tribes of the interior. It was the last link with the past and therefore the last thing with which the clan was willing to part.[43]

The author of the article was Louis Shotridge, himself a Tlingit. A tall and attractive man, who had toured with

---

43. Louis Shotridge, "Ghost of Courageous Adventurer," *Museum Journal* 11, no. 1 (March 1920): 11–12.

an Indian opera company and was said to have a fine tenor voice,[44] Shotridge (1882–1937) came from a prominent and noble family in the community of Klukwan, Alaska, and had attended a Presbyterian missionary school in nearby Haines. From an early age he showed versatility, an ability to move between the traditional world of the Tlingit and the modern culture of the United States, which Alaska had joined as a district in 1867. This ability was key to

44. Douglas Cole, *Captured Heritage: The Scramble for Northwest Coast Artifacts* (Seattle: University of Washington Press, 1985), p. 256.

the remarkable role he played in the relationship between the native peoples of his region and American archaeology. More than seventy years after his death, his legacy continues to be debated among ethnologists and his own people. It may never be entirely resolved, but its complexity can be better appreciated within the context of the peculiar historical, social, and cultural events of his time.

The 1905 Lewis and Clark Centennial Exposition in Portland, Oregon, was the event that launched his career. His wife, the strikingly beautiful Florence Dennis, an accomplished weaver of Chilkat baskets, was invited to the exposition to perform a demonstration of her craft, and Shotridge, then twenty-three, accompanied her with the purpose of selling a few Tlingit artifacts. George Byron Gordon, then curator and eventually director of the University Museum, was one of his customers. Gordon, an ambitious director and collector, was determined to put the museum on the map, and by most assessments he did—quickly building a vast collection and fundraising for an expansion of the building. Gordon became director of the University Museum in 1910, in a key period of expansion of American museums that created a frantic race to collect historical artifacts. In this climate, large-budget institutions fiercely competed against each other to get their hands on the greatest amount of collectible items possible.

Shotridge and Gordon were very taken by each other. Gordon saw in Shotridge a young, energetic, smart, and eager (although inexperienced) conduit to the riches of the Pacific Northwest. Shotridge saw in Gordon a mentor and a bridge to modern American society. Shotridge did

not have a formal education in ethnology or anthropology, but after some years of trading with Gordon he received three years of training at the University Museum before being made assistant curator there in 1915. He was quickly exposed to some of the greatest minds of the fields of linguistics, ethnology, and anthropology. In 1912, through the help of anthropologist Frank Speck, he and Dennis met the Canadian linguist Edward Sapir, with whom they worked, providing information and objects. In 1914 they met Franz Boas, considered the father of modern anthropology. Gordon arranged for Shotridge to attend Boas's lectures in New York, and as a result Boas worked with Shotridge to develop the first record of Tlingit phonology. Boas's training was essential to Shotridge, who learned processes of recording and other methods to conduct research that were key in his later work in the museum. He was exacting in his record keeping and correspondence, a quality today's researchers are grateful for. He was a competent writer, and he produced several articles for the *Museum Journal*, such as "Ghost of Courageous Adventurer," in which he simultaneously described ethnographic objects and traditions and revealed anecdotal information about himself. One of his early assignments, a scale model of the central section of the village of Klukwan, was so painstakingly produced that it continues to be a prized component of the museum's exhibits.

Shotridge truly believed in the necessity of salvaging and documenting the traditions of his people. In 1923 he wrote, "It is clear that unless someone go[es] to work [to] record our history in the English language and place these old things as evidence, the noble idea of our forefathers shall be entirely lost."[45] Over the course of his career, Shotridge collected more than five hundred items for the University Museum. While not astronomical in quantity, the quality of the objects he obtained is extraordinary and they constitute one of the great collections in the world of such material. Shotridge had a unique advantage over competing collectors; being a native speaker of Tlingit, familiar with local cultural codes and the region in general,

---

45. Shotridge, quoted in Lucy Fowler Williams, "Louis Shotridge: Preserver of Tlingit History," in Sergei Kan and Steve Henrikson, eds., *Sharing Our Knowledge* (forthcoming).

he knew where to look for valuable items and was likely more trusted by their owners.

There is a darker side to Shotridge's legacy that is often highlighted by some ethnologists. He appeared to be extremely eager to satisfy the demands of Gordon and the museum in obtaining objects and performing—symbolically and literally—the role of native interpreter for institutional and pedagogical purposes. Shotridge and Dennis became living interpreters of Native American customs in general, not just those of the Pacific Northwest. In one of the most frequently reproduced photographs of the couple, they are wearing outfits that appear more appropriate for Buffalo Bill's Wild West show than Alaska. Of their reenactments, ethnologist Elizabeth P. Seaton has written,

> What is striking about these public performances are their acts of miming alterity. Playing to oth-ers' expectations as to what constitutes Indianness, the Shotridges are held to enact Anglo-American

desires for a pure, unsullied order of origin in a world which has come undone. In this respect, the two (in) authentic Indians are posed against the degenerate hybridities of an industrialized modernity.[46]

The extent to which Shotridge was an "(in)authentic" performer or an instrument to satisfy expectations for whites about "the other" is debatable. What is clear, however, is that Shotridge was a talented recorder and mimicker of behavior, and he employed this ability to perform himself and his culture for white audiences and to portray the traditions of whites for his own people. In the article "My Northland Revisited," Shotridge described a visit to his ancestral land and his decision to organize an "evening story telling league" there, in Haines:

> The main object of the organization was to impress on the minds of the modern Indian children the former life of the tribe to which they belong. For my part I told of my observations on life among the Caucasians and the customs and habits of other progressive races.

In the nearby town of Wrangell, he wrote, he gave a talk "on the modern life in the progressive world of the white man." About that event Shotridge added,

> It was obvious that the younger people, most of whom are half white, are very much fascinated by the ways

---

46. Elizabeth P. Seaton, "The Native Collector: Louis Shotridge and the Contests of Possession," *Ethnography*, no. 2 (2001): 47.

and language of the white people and as a result had organized a society called "The Alaska Brotherhood," which is said to have been originated somewhere farther north as "The Alaska Native Brotherhood." Since the middle adjective "native" conflicts with their ambition to become white men, it was necessary for the Klawaks to omit it. Apparently the organization was well represented at the meeting, as I had all that I could do to come through with a talk on "Preservation of natural character."[47]

Through these brief descriptions of educational and social events we can form an image of how Shotridge negotiated his own fractured identity and how he helped others articulate the negotiation between cultures. He considered it important to integrate native and colonial culture so both sides could get to know each other. He particularly wanted those who shared his native heritage to have the opportunity to integrate into what he described as "the progressive world" of United States collective culture. It was that "progressive world" that drove him to obtain more and more material from his people, and he found himself maintaining a social standing in one world through what he could obtain from the other.

Shotridge's detractors usually zero in on one particular issue: his failed acquisition of the spectacular Klukwan Whale House collection. Shotridge had always been keen to obtain this collection—an ornate house screen and various posts—for the museum, but the community was

---

47. Shotridge, "My Northland Revisited," *Museum Journal* 8, 2 (1917): 105–15.

reluctant to let it go. In 1922 he lobbied for its acquisition, offering $3,500 to the community, but the offer was rejected. Shotridge had a direct familiar connection with this house, as his father, Yeilgooxú, had been its headman. After Yeilgooxú's death, the community had decided that the title should be passed to the headman of the Raven House instead of the customary heir, Shotridge's uncle, who was considered unfit. Shotridge convinced his uncle to contest the headmanship of the house, and using American laws he laid claim to the property as the son of Yeilgooxú. The community was profoundly divided over the issue, so much so that a special peace ceremony was organized to calm down the various factions. Shotridge was aware of the havoc he was causing, but that did not deter him from making another attempt at taking the house posts and screens in July 1923, an attempt that also failed. In the end he gave up, expressing regret later for this episode of his life, but the controversy continues to haunt his legacy.

Shotridge's last decade of life was painful. Gordon died in 1927, falling from the stairs of the Racquet Club in Philadelphia, and Shotridge lost his main supporter at the museum and a friend of many years. Shortly after, in 1928, his second wife, Elizabeth Cook, died of tuberculosis. (Margaret Dennis had also died of tuberculosis, in 1917, and he had married Elizabeth, another Tlinglit Indian, in 1919.) Shotridge spent a good deal of his savings taking care of his wife and providing for their three children. He did remarry once more, in the early 1930s, to another Tlingit, Mary Kassan, with whom he had two more children, and he was elected president of the Alaska Native Brotherhood camp in Sitka. The Great Depression affected the ability of the city of Philadelphia to make its annual appropriations to the museum, and in 1931 Shotridge's pay was cut by fifteen percent and in 1932 was eliminated altogether. Shotridge, in his fifties, went back to Alaska, cut off from the south, unable to do the only job he had been trained to do. In 1935 he took the job of fishing guard in Sitka—a government position that locals resented, as he was in charge of preventing the illegal fishing that many there saw as vital to their sustenance. It was there that Shotridge met his end, a death that has been the subject of much controversy. He was found on the ground in Redoubt Bay, where he had been lying for several days, injured. He was taken to a hospital in Sitka where he died of a broken neck. According to the official story, his death was the result of an accidental fall. Others theorized that a poacher Shotridge had recently ordered off the river had taken revenge, and there were rumors that other enemies—or the spirits—had sought retribution for his extracting of sacred objects from his people. What is certain is that Louis Shotridge, the first Pacific Northwest Indian to ever work in a museum, the first recorder of Tlingit grammar, the ethnographer, performer, translator, and traveler, died in an undignified way, destitute and largely forgotten.

* * *

In 2001, more than half a century later, Suzanna Urminska, a student at the University of Pennsylvania, became interested in a group of five hundred photographs that had lain semi-forgotten in a corner of the University Museum's archive. They are pictures taken by Shotridge, depicting all sorts of aspects of the customs and traditions of the Tlingit. She decided to go to Klukwan with the pictures to research their historical and family connections.

The reaction to her visit and to the photographs was something Urminska could not have anticipated. She unexpectedly reopened an unhealed wound—the controversial legacy of Louis Shotridge. While some in the local tribal council appreciated the value of the pictures and even recognized family members in them, others would not mention Shotridge by name. Urminska was accused of naïveté and a lack of sensitivity to a painful episode. An article in the *Anchorage Daily News* described the restitution of the photographs as a reminder of what Shotridge took from the Tlingit:

> A potlatch hat or a clan house panel is a powerful object, an *at.óow*. *At.óow* are objects so finely interwoven with clan history, experience, life and ancestry that many are given names and are kept active in the culture and in their lineage. To separate an *at.oow* from Tlingit people for "preservation" is rather like cutting someone's healthy arm for posterity. The body is terribly harmed.[48]

The article ultimately suggests that painful memories be left alone. No mention is made of the photographs themselves, which are not artifacts but records available to all and, regardless of who had taken them, valuable historical documents. It was only because the photographs had been made by Shotridge that many could not see the value in them.

* * *

Shotridge's writings display a sincere concern for the preservation of culture. There is a sense of urgency in his reports, as if he knew that the pace of modernity was quickly wiping out the world he had come from. His attempts at mediation, such as the promotion of oral history, may have not been sufficient, but they feel sincere.

---

48. Diane Benson, "Superficial Treatment of a Sensitive History," *Anchorage Daily News*, July 22, 2001.

Seaton's judgment of Shotridge strikes me as extremely harsh. In her interpretation, filtered through postcolonial theory, he was an "(in)authentic" mimicker of otherness, someone who, in a Faustian bargain that haunted him to his death, lost himself and his people to the predatory hunger of white collectors. It is hard to deny that there was a certain narcissism in his enterprises, that he sounds boisterous and even arrogant in his claims in early letters to Gordon that only he could find the treasures that would salvage the culture of his people. He also seems to mimic Gordon in his ambition, and the underlying sentiment in all his projects appears, ultimately, to be a desire for acceptance among the "progressive society" of the whites, and when confronted with either/or propositions, it seems he turned his back to his people. But he was not a cynic. He was torn, conflicted about his constant negotiation between cultures. Those who have been there, between two systems of logic, know that to take sides is impossible. In the end, one floats in a void between two realities. Shotridge was in a very lonely position, which must have become even lonelier once he was cut off from the museum and alienated from his people.

Most importantly, the accusation of inauthenticity presupposes the possibility of an "authentic performance" in the unusual circumstances Shotridge had to navigate. Had he never left his village and never learned English, he may have remained an "authentic" native, but instead he had to navigate an uncharted territory of identity. He may not have always made the best decisions, but many of the ones he did make, like the taking of those photographs, the transcription of myths and narratives, and the Tlingit grammar and recordings have ensured that knowledge of his culture endures, unlike other cultures who had no Shotridge to preserve their physical and immaterial heritage.

* * *

In order to better understand the story Shotridge left behind to those closest to him, I contacted his family members. One of them was Israel Shotridge, an artist and grand-nephew of Louis Shotridge. Israel and his wife, Sue, were in New York for an exhibition at the Museum of the American Indian, where Israel was exhibiting some of his celebrated traditional carvings. I took them for a drink before they went to see the *Lion King*.

"I was fixated by Louis, even before I knew he was my uncle," Israel said. He had discovered that he was related to Shotridge only when he was in college. Of his relatives, Israel is the only one who has taken the last name Shotridge, causing some tensions among the family (they all have kept the Jackson last name), and the legacy of the grand-uncle still generates mixed reactions among them. Israel, in contrast, has chosen to embrace it. "Shotridge" is an anglicized Tlingit version of *Shaadaxhícht*, the name of Louis's maternal grandfather. "You know, the government, they try to erase your name, your history, history that you and I should know about," Israel said.

I asked him if the rumors about foul play in Louis's death were true.

"If you lived in Alaska, you would know," he said, smiling, and took a sip of his beer.

* * *

The Tlingit narrative "Ghost of Courageous Adventurer," which discloses the origin of the dagger in the University Museum's collection, is "poetic in form and often archaic," Shotridge wrote. Using strange and fascinating expressions such as "fire was dropped" (to mean that a break was taken for lunch) and "but man's face-impression there was none" (to describe an uninhabited place), the semi-epic tale describes how the ancestral explorers of Klukwan heroically crossed inhospitable lands, losing many through cold and starvation, to reach another village. In the process they discovered iron and ivory—commemorated in the materials in the dagger.[49]

Shotridge once wrote, "Only through sacrifice does man acquire something of value. It was at the cost of brave lives that we now have in our hands those objects that now constitute our pride."[50] One is left to wonder if Shotridge himself, in his last agonizing hours on that river shore, reviewed the events of his life, and if he thought about his personal sacrifices in obtaining those objects—if he saw in himself, for a moment, the ghost of the courageous adventurer.

---

49. Shotridge, "Ghost of Corageous Adventurer," pp. 11–14.
50. Shotridge, quoted in Norah Marks Dauenhauer, *Native American Voices on Identity, Art and Culture: Objects of Everlasting Value* (Philadelphia: University Museum of Archaeology and Anthropology, 2005), p. 139.

V. The Pearl in the Mouth of

the Last Chinese Empress

The Empress Dowager of China was one of the
most famous rulers in the history of the Orient.
This photograph was taken by an American woman
artist who painted her portrait.

"MAY YOU FIND what you are looking for" is said to be the third and most damning of a group of ancient Chinese curses. That the phrase, popularized in the West through English-speaking diplomats in China in the 1930s, sounds positive makes it the more ominous; it hints that unwished consequences will come to those who are overly eager or ambitious—like the protagonist couple of W.W. Jacob's 1902 horror story "The Monkey's Paw," whose wish for money is fulfilled by way of the death of their son in the army.

On November 15, 1908, the last empress of China died after nearly a half-century on the throne. The reign of Empress Dowager Cixi, one of the longest ruling female monarchs in history, had not been a happy one. She had reached power through manipulation and intrigue, after giving birth to the only male heir of the Xiangfeng Emperor. Her son, the Tonxzhi Emperor, and, later, her nephew, the Guangxu Emperor, ruled China nominally while she was the de facto ruler. Many attribute the decline and eventual fall of the Qing Dynasty and the advent of the Chinese Revolution to her behind-the-scenes rule.

Upon her death, a pearl was put inside her mouth. In Chinese mortuary custom, the pearl was meant to protect the body from decomposition and also to provide the deceased with a means to bribe his or her judges in the other world. Empress Cixi's pearl, however, was no ordinary one: it was the size of a robin's egg. She was known for her fondness for jewels, and her treasure included three thousand boxes of "everyday jewels." She was buried in a tomb of her own design along with her rich possessions.

But the empress had no rest after death. Twenty years later, in 1928 her tomb was occupied and ransacked by the forces of Sun Dianying, a Chinese warlord of the Kuomintang. Opening the grave, they took out the jadeite watermelon, lotus, and coral jewelry, the imperial robe, the shoes, and all the precious stones on the body. As an ultimate indignity, the looters opened the Empress's mouth and extracted the giant pearl. Rumor has it that it ended decorating the party shoes of Chiang Kai-shek's wife, Soong May-Ling, who showed it off on special occasions. No one knows its whereabouts today.

* * *

A few months before the theft, on the other side of the world the director of the University Museum, George Byron Gordon, received a letter from Eldridge A. Johnson, the founder of the Victor Talking Machine Company and one of the most reliable museum board members and benefactors. Johnson mentioned that he had seen and been fascinated by "a large rock crystal globe" at the John Wanamaker's store in Philadelphia, which he wanted to buy for himself. The fifty-five-pound ball, Johnson wrote, "is ten inches in diameter, silver white and perfect in every way . . . The Wanamakers claim that it once belonged to the Dowager Empress. It was, I believe, for some time located in the Imperial Palace at Pekin." The price of the sphere was $50,000 (today $620,000). Johnson concluded, "I would like very much to talk to you about it. Would it

be convenient for you to meet me at some club during the later part of this week or next week?"[51]

Gordon was a highly respected scholar and successful director, "whose personality was as sharp as the long needles of his waxed moustache," Percy Madeira wrote in a history of the museum.[52] Since his appointment to the

---

51. Eldridge A. Johnson, letter to George Byron Gordon, University Museum Archives.
52. Percy C. Madeira, *Men in Search of Man: The First Seventy-Five Years of the University Museum of the University of Pennsylvania* (Philadelphia: University of Pennsylvania Press, 1964), p. 30.

directorship in 1910, he had overseen the largest expansion in the history of the University Museum, and he was renowned for his collector's eye and his connoisseurship; many of the best items in the collection came to the museum during Gordon's tenure—including the Pacific Northwest objects he secured through Louis Shotridge. He lived during an unprecedented—and highly unlikely to be repeated—era of personal wealth and institutional ambition that to our eyes looks like unchecked arrogance. The resources of American philanthropists seemed unlimited, and in a frenetic competition with European museums that had the advantage of centuries of colonization, cultural entrepreneurs and museum board members collected at a furious pace. Issues of provenance were not as pressing as they are now, and records of how certain items arrived in certain collections of that era are imperfect at best.

Gordon had a special interest in Chinese artifacts. In 1913, to inaugurate the museum's new rotunda, he had pushed for a spectacular exhibition of Chinese art. Entailing multiple donations and purchases of ancient items, it became known as "the first million-dollar show."[53] Gordon's tenure was later characterized as the museum's Chinese Period.

We don't know whether Gordon and Johnson had that conversation, but it is likely that Gordon immediately wanted the Dowager Empress, as the crystal sphere became known, for the museum. It would have been a crowning item for its already spectacular Chinese collection. A few

53. Dilys Pegler Winegrand, *Through Time, Across Continents: A Hundred Years of Archaeology and Anthropology at the University Museum* (Philadelphia: University of Pennsylvania Press, 1993), p. 61.

days after receiving Johnson's letter, Gordon attended
an event at the Racquet Club of Philadelphia and dined
with the Roosevelt brothers, Theodore, Jr., and Kermit.
He slipped walking up a marble stair, struck his head,
and died six hours later. In memoriam, Johnson gave the
museum a collection of Chinese objects—including the
Dowager Empress.

A 1929 article in *Mentor Magazine* describes the new
acquisition: "Imagine if you can a jewel of fifty pounds
weight, so beautifully cut and polished and with so exqui-
site a shimmer of shadow and light that it appears a ball
of almost gossamer fragility." The article concludes with
a discussion of crystal's mystical attributes: "The Hindus
made the practice of reading the future from crystals an
elaborate art . . . and there are many people of the present
day that believe the practice of 'scrying' is not as unre-
warding as the unsuperstitious would have us believe."[54]
Whatever powers the Dowager Empress may have, no
one predicted that it would have a traveling life of its own,
like the giant pearl's afterlife in the high-society parties
of Taiwan, on the shoe of Soong May-Ling. For years
after the passing of Gordon and Johnson, the Dowager
Empress was the most popular object at the University
Museum and was on display in the place of honor—the
center of the Chinese Rotunda Gordon had inaugurated
with the "million-dollar" Chinese show.

The museum has a complex system of motion-detector
alarms and monitors. On November 11, 1988, a guard
started his shift at 8:15 p.m.; when, around 2 a.m., an

54. J. Leroy Miller, "A Giant Jewel of China," *Mentor Magazine*
(January 1929): 30.

alarm sounded, he assumed it had been triggered by a group of painters working in the museum that night. It was not until 8:15 a.m. that he noticed that the glass case protecting the Dowager Empress had been shattered and the precious object and its ornate base were gone. A door at the museum's Spruce and Thirty-third Streets entrance was damaged, and a valuable Egyptian figure of Osiris was also missing.

The director of the museum, Robert H. Dyson, was devastated. He felt, he said, "like a sacrificial victim from ancient Mexico" whose heart had been cut out "and thrown down the stairs of the temple."[55] Despite the uproar and an FBI investigation, no traces were found—the thieves had done an efficient job. Weeks, months, and years went by, the trail grew cold, and hopes of recovery dwindled.

The Dowager Empress was likely the last thing on Jes Camby's mind on October 24, 1991, as she walked into the South Street Garage Sale pawnshop just across the Schuylkill River from the University Museum. Camby, a researcher at the museum and a former curator of ancient Near Eastern art, was browsing for a mirror and a table for her house when she encountered a familiar object—a bronze statue of Osiris. Camby immediately recognized the artifact and hastily fetched museum curators. It turned out the shopkeeper had bought the statue from a homeless man named Al for thirty dollars. Al, in turn, led the authorities to Lawrence Stametz, a bookkeeper in his early thirties who lived in West Mount Airy. The month of

55. Robert H. Dyson, quoted in Gabriel Escobar, "Penn Museum Crystal Ball, Statue Stolen Guard Ignored Burglar Alarms," *Philadelphia Daily News*, November 12, 1988.

the theft, Stametz, going through a number of cardboard boxes in his garage, had found the old statue and crystal ball inside one of them. He thought the statue "was kind of ugly" and the ball looked "like an alien egg."[56]

When he moved homes, he gave the Osiris statue to Al as a gift. And where was the crystal ball? Stametz had given it to his housekeeper, Kim Beckles, as a birthday present. Beckles thought it was a fun thing. At her home in Trenton she had placed it on a coffee table on top of a metal dish that she used for flower arrangements. However, she reported, "the same day I was talking on the phone and the sun came through the crystal ball and burned my arm," so she moved it to an upstairs bedroom away from the sunlight. A year later, FBI agents knocked on

56. Lawrence Stametz, quoted in Edward Colimore, "He Found the Artifacts, and They Were Ugly," *Philadelphia Inquirer,* November 1, 1991.

her door and asked if they could take a look at a certain item in her possession.

* * *

A superstitious reader, or a fan of *Raiders of the Lost Ark* with a hyperactive imagination, may piece together the loose threads I have outlined here into a screenplay: the magical crystal ball, snatched away from its original palace, had absorbed the spirit of the Dowager Empress Cixi. Gordon's accidental death led to the museum's ownership of the object he desired, ironically fulfilling the ancient Chinese curse "May you find what you are looking for." In the desecration of the Empress's tomb, the sphere had been condemned to wander away from its owner, like the pearl taken from her mouth. The corollary of the Chinese curse: If you find, you are also bound to lose.

Except—the Chinese curse is likely a foreigner's invention. There is no document from outside the English-speaking world proving that the phrase originated in ancient Chinese wisdom. We only have the verbal recollections of foreign diplomats, prone to mistranslation and unintended fabrication through faulty memory or misunderstanding. Similarly, the authenticity of the crystal sphere can't be unequivocally traced to the Dowager Empress Cixi. According to the original brochure describing it, the object had traveled for several years before it finally arrived in the hands of the Wanamakers, who brought it to Philadelphia. Even if such an object belonged to the Empress, we don't know if she held it in her hands—she was known to have thousands of precious objects. We may never know its true origins. But in the meantime this crystal sphere, which at different times has been worth half a million dollars and nothing, which has been both a coffee-table ornament and an imperial treasure, stands today in the middle of the Chinese Rotunda, still a centerpiece of the mighty Chinese collection Gordon built, waiting perhaps to one day live yet another life.

VI. The Creatures of Acámbaro

ONE AFTERNOON IN 1944, a German businessman named Waldemar Julsrud, hiking on the Cerro del Toro, a hill near the town of Acámbaro in Guanajuato, Mexico, spotted a strange object on the ground. It looked like an ancient ceramic figurine, and Julsrud, a collector with an interest in pre-Columbian cultures, was impressed by his find. Back at home he asked one of his assistants—Odilón Tinajero, a local laborer—to search for more in the area and bring them to him.

Odilón returned a few days later with a number of extraordinary specimens—figures made in hard clay. Fascinated, Julsrud asked Odilón to do an even more thorough search, offering to pay him a peso per piece (at the time, minimum wage in Mexico was ten pesos a month). He was a demanding collector: to ensure that Odilón would excavate as carefully as possible, he speci-fied that he would not pay for broken pieces. A few days later Odilón brought a cache of objects even more vast and exotic, with lots of complete pieces. And so it continued: dozens of items were delivered every week, totaling hun-dreds every month, demonstrating that Odilón's innate talents for detection and excavation surpassed those of the most capable archaeologists.

Mexican archaeologists had begun to uncover Chupícuaro artifacts (dating as early as 400 B.C.) in that region in 1926, likely after Julsrud had moved to the area. Archaeologists Enrique Juan Palacios and later Ramon Mena and Porfirio Aguirre made the first discoveries of Chupícuaro pottery, and it was the subject of a variety of archaeological stud-ies in the 1940s and 1950s. Many of the pieces Odilón

delivered were formally similar to the ancient artifacts usually found in that region, but others had no characteristics tying them with Chupícuaro, Tarascan, or any other known Mesoamerican culture. Their thematic range seemed to encompass the fauna of the whole world, including images of sea horses, turtles, anteaters, llamas, and camels; complex architectural structures such as fountains; strange social scenes such as a man playing with a giant monkey; women flirting with reptiles; and animals with six arms—all unlike any ancient representations seen before. Moreover, their aesthetic references were extremely diverse, suggesting anything from an Egyptian influence (there were sarcophagi-like pieces) to elements of Hinduism and African cultures. Every new object added to the evidence showing Julsrud that he had found the most ancient of cultures at Cerro del Toro. In addition, that incredible

collection contained one particularly perplexing group of items: ceramic figures of animals from the Mesozoic era, such as a brontosaurus, trachodon, tyrannosaurus, and plesiosaurus, playfully running with human figures. The historical implications of such depictions, Julsrud must have reckoned, were profound. That was the beginning of the Julsrud collection, which, thanks to the reliability of Odilón's searching techniques, reached a total of thirty-seven thousand pieces.

Waldemar Julsrud was born in Bremen, Germany, in 1875. He immigrated to Mexico in 1896, like many other

Europeans, as part of an immigration initiative of the pro-European dictator of Mexico, Porfirio Díaz. When the Mexican Revolution started—with the objective of toppling Díaz and his collaborators—Julsrud moved from Mexico City to Acámbaro. The quiet little town is located in the southeastern part of the state of Guanajuato and is mainly known for its bakeries, which make a type of white leavened bread similar to Jewish *challah*. There Julsrud set up a hardware shop, La Reina, the largest business in the main square, and developed an active interest in archaeology.

Sometime after Odilón's exciting discoveries, Julsrud started to publicize his findings. In 1947 he self-published an archaeological text of his, titled *"Enigmas del pasado"* (Enigmas of the past), which he distributed to the press. Apparently the *New York Times* and the BBC ignored his overtures, but in 1948 the Mexican daily *Excelsior* published an article about his collection: "The Primitives Who Lived in Mexico Knew the Antediluvian Animals."[57]

57. Quoted by Lowell Harmer in "Mexico Finds Give Hint of Lost World," *Los Angeles Times*, March 25, 1951.

There is no positive evidence showing how the archaeo-logical community in Mexico reacted to the news, but the lack of follow-up publications suggests that it was with incredulity or indifference. Fortunately for Julsrud, a non-Mexican reporter became interested. His name was Lowell Harmer, then an information officer for a joint United States–Mexico commission. Julsrud visited Harmer in his office in Mexico City. The latter later described the encounter: "His blue eyes twinkled with excitement as he unwrapped two dinosaur statues and placed them on my desk. 'You are looking at the oldest man-made things on this earth.' His voice was confident and sincere. 'These ceramics were made 100,000,000 years ago by men who lived in the same era with the giant reptiles.' "[58] Harmer pointed out that anthropologists believe that man evolved only 500,000 years ago and dinosaurs existed around

58. Ibid.

100,000,000 B.C., but Julsrud confidently dismissed the notion, defiantly inviting any archaeologist to examine his collection.

On March 25, 1951, Harmer published an article in the *Los Angeles Times* titled "Mexico Finds Give Hint of Lost World: Dinosaur Statues Point to Men Who Lived in Age of Reptiles."[59] By that time there was a buzz around the so-called "Julsrud people." Another journalist, William N. Russell of Los Angeles, became interested in the collection. He became one of its main supporters in the United States and lobbied for it to gain coverage.

The next year, the Amerind Foundation, a renowned American archaeological organization, took upon itself the task of a scientific study of the Julsrud collection. Archaeologist and researcher Charles C. Di Peso traveled

---

59. Ibid.

to Acámbaro to examine the objects, and he published his conclusions in an article in *American Antiquity* in April 1952.[60] Di Peso's study was a thorough and devastating refutation of the authenticity of the collection. He enumerated a long list of problems with the pieces, starting with the obvious: the thousands of objects had been found in the same area, excavated, and restored by the same inexperienced person; there was no patination on the objects or the coating of soluble salts that characterizes authentic figures from the region; the locations and forms of the cracks in some of the figures showed that they had been intentionally broken, and none of the surfaces had been worn smooth—meaning that they had been recently broken. Likely due to his professionalism, Di Peso refrained from saying the obvious: the pieces all *looked* absurdly fake. He had followed Odilón and his son and watched them excavate at the site for two days. On the second day, when Odilón found a cache of objects, Di Peso verified that the type of earth in the section where the figurines were lying was a mixture of contemporary soil—he even saw fresh manure—with older red earth, which meant that the pieces had been carelessly planted. He dryly concluded his report by adding, "Further investigation revealed that a family living in the vicinity of Acámbaro make these figurines during the winter months when their fields lie idle."[61]

Di Peso's article must have been a bitter pill for Julsrud to swallow. In conversations with others, he thoroughly

60. Charles C. Di Peso, "The Clay Figurines of Acámbaro, Guanajuato, Mexico," *American Antiquity* 18, no. 4 (April 1953): 388–89.
61. Ibid.

dismissed Di Peso's study. He said that Di Peso had only spent a few hours examining the collection—which was true—and that when he had not succeeded in acquiring pieces from the collection he had decided to discredit it. (It is possible that Di Peso had wished to purchase authentic Chupícuaro objects or that he feigned interest in purchasing archaeological items so that he would be directed, as he claimed he eventually was, to the house of a family who made "Julsrud-like" items.)

The study and Julsrud's noise led the archaeologists of Mexico's Instituto Nacional de Antropología e Historia (INAH) to conduct their own excavation, to settle the issue once and for all, in 1954. The INAH comprised some of the most prominent Mexican archaeologists at the time, Eduardo Noguera Auza, Rafael Orellana, Ponciano Salazar Ortegón, and José Antonio Pompa y Pompa. By this time, the appearance of the controversial objects had changed life in the sleepy town of Acámbaro, and a lot seemed to be at stake. The townsfolk surrounded the area chosen for excavation, near the Cerro del Toro, to observe. As the excavation proceeded, the archaeologists found the usual fragments of Tarascan or Chupícuaro ceramic and what appeared to be a tooth of a horse from the Ice Age, but no ceramic objects similar to those in the Julsrud collection. In their final report, the Mexican archaeologists came to the same conclusion as Di Peso: "This is a case of reproduction, that is, falsification, made fairly recently."[62] And like he had done with Di Peso, Julsrud spun the claims of the Mexican archaeologists, saying that they had told

---

62. Eduardo Noguera, "Report of the INAH Expedition" (University Museum Archives, 1954).

him in private that the pieces were authentic, and that they had changed their story as soon as they returned to Mexico City.

After this, the case was considered closed by the archaeology world, but Julsrud did not accept the judgment of the experts on a matter that had become his mission in life: to prove that the mother of all cultures, more ancient than any other by hundreds of millions of years, had existed near the doorstep of his house in Acámbaro.

In 1955, Arthur M. Young of Philadelphia, a helicopter inventor who held unorthodox views about the evolution of humankind, became interested in the Julsrud collection. Young (who later created The Foundation for the Study of Consciousness) sent a researcher to Mexico to make a full study of the collection and he proposed an exhibition of the Julsrud materials to the University Museum in Philadelphia.

Young's researcher was Charles H. Hapgood, a historian with a degree in medieval and modern history from Harvard. While he had no background as an archaeologist, his academic standing gave him, at least, a bit more credibility than Julsrud. Hapgood visited Julsrud, who by this time had barely room for his own bed in his nine-room house packed with thousands upon thousands of artifacts. (He was later reported to be sleeping in his bathtub, after completely running out of space.) Hapgood attempted an excavation of his own in an area where Julsrud said artifacts had been discovered. He found no figures but did uncover a few fragments of ceramic. That was enough evidence for him, and he became one of the most fervent advocates of the authenticity of the Julsrud collection.

Charles Hapgood (seventh from left) with Waldemar Julsrud (fourth from left) and Odilón Tinajero (second from left), in Acámbaro, 1955.

Froelich Rainey, then director of the University Museum, thought that the debate around the contested items would make a compelling exhibition. Linton Satterthwaite, the curator given the task of organizing the show, apparently did not agree. In correspondence and in exhibition labels he made it clear that he considered the whole story a sham. Nonetheless, he proceeded dutifully with the job at hand, and a selection of Julsrud pieces traveled to the museum in 1955. After looking at the comics available in the region and the movies at the local cinema, Di Peso had theorized that locals had made the pieces after looking at the comics available in the region and the movies at the local cinema. Satterthwaite included Mexican magazines in the exhibition to show American audiences that a Mexican villager in 1945 would know what a dinosaur looked like. It didn't occur to Satterthwaite to mention, or perhaps he didn't know, that the first natural history museum in the Americas had been founded in Mexico City in 1790, when the United States was fourteen years old. In fact, natural history expeditions took place in Mexico in 1571, before the arrival of the *Mayflower*, as the Spanish collected specimens for the examination of the royal courts, and dinosaurs were exhibited in Mexico City as early as 1928, with the donation by Andrew Carnegie's widow of a replica of the *Diplodocus Carnegiei* to what is known today as the Museo del Chopo.

Diplodocus carnegiei at the Museo del Chopo, Mexico City, c. 1928.

Julsrud died in 1964 in León, Mexico, leaving his family with quite a legacy of objects. Odilón vanished around that time, and no one seems to have heard from him again. The mystery behind the creatures of Acámbaro continued. Hapgood went back to Mexico in 1968 to conduct more investigations, and shortly after that, in 1972, Young arranged for three samples of the Acámbaro materials to be examined in Philadelphia, by the new method of dating artifacts developed at the University Museum. The method, known as thermoluminescence, consists in calculating the amount of time since a particular crystalline material (a sample from the object in question) had been last heated, thus determining, for ceramic, when it had been fired. The results of the sampling, reported by Rainey in a letter, were surprising: the materials were thousands of years old. This, to Hapgood and his supporters, was the final proof that the objects were authentic. The University Museum found itself in the awkward position of either confirming the pieces as authentic—contradicting most other evidence—or admitting that the test was faulty. Rainey did give one qualification to the results, which Hapgood ignored: "Our lab comments that to give accurate thermoluminescence dates, the pottery would have to be fired above 500 degrees centigrade. The three figurines analyzed might not have been fired to that degree of heat, which could explain an error."[63] It was also possible that the samples had been taken not from the dinosaur figures but from other, authenticated ceramics from Chupícuaro.

In 1973 Hapgood self-published *Mystery in Acámbaro*, a grand report in which he traced a history of the discovery of the pieces, arguing that they were unquestionably authentic and finding every possible way to discredit Di Peso and every other critic. Hapgood had an elaborate and creative explanation for every one of Di Peso's objections: Di Peso could not have examined every single object; during his site visit, he had studied an area that had been disturbed because Odilón had been teaching children to excavate earlier that day, and for that reason he had indeed planted the items Di Peso saw him dig up; Odilón had washed

---

63. Froelich Rainey, quoted in Charles H. Hapgood, *Mystery in Acámbaro* (Brattleboro, Vt.: self-published, 1973), p. 10.

the figurines and so no residue was left on them; Di Peso had ulterior motives for discrediting the collection; and so forth. He argued that the pieces, if they were fakes, would have to have been baked in an open oven, which would have been impossible to conceal in the town. Of particular interest in Hapgood's and other subsequent pro-Julsrud studies is the ambiguous description of Odilón Tinajero. They defend the authenticity of the relics by describing him as an ignorant, illiterate villager, incapable of forging a clay figurine; yet he is credited with the discovery of nearly forty thousand items over the course of a few years, almost all intact, the feat of a supernaturally gifted archaeologist. As in so many old-time colonialist narratives, the protagonists are the enlightened white explorers, while the locals remain anonymous, in the background.

Hapgood ended his study with a description of the University Museum's dating experiments, concluding, "With these tests, the case rests."[64] In 1978, however, a new study proved that thermoluminescence dating was inaccurate, concluding, once more, that the Julsrud collection was fake. And despite Hapgood's arguments, Di Pesos's original objections were not disproven: it would have been impossible for the inexperienced Julsrud or Odilón to have cleaned every single object in acid, eliminating all vestiges of age; and Acámbaro is a town of large old ovens—the clay pieces may have been baked next to loaves of Acámbaro bread, at less than five hundred degrees.

Hapgood was killed in a car accident in 1982, and with his death the collection lost its most important advocate. The pieces ended up in the possession of the municipality

64. Hapgood, *Mystery*, p. 10.

of Acámbaro, which, apparently unsure about what to do with them, kept them in storage for several years. For a while it seemed that the Julsrud collection would vanish into obscurity.

In the 1990s, however, a new wave of people went to Acámbaro to again try to solve the mystery of the figurines. Several American Creationists, in search of proof that humans and dinosaurs coexisted, became aware of the artifacts. One of them, Dr. Dennis Swift, was instrumental in bringing the artifacts out of storage, although by that time many of them had disappeared. Swift photographed the entire existing collection, and he maintains a website where he argues for its authenticity.

Swift lobbied local authorities and the state government of Guanajuato to recognize the importance of the collection. At a press conference in Acámbaro in 1999 he distributed T-shirts with images of dinosaurs, suggesting the touristic viability of the collection. Swift's efforts paid off: in 2002 the Museo Waldemar Julsrud opened to the public in Acámbaro. Typical of Mexican local government projects, the museum provides more spectacle than education. Its meager official website has a description full of factual errors, quoting, predictably, only people like Hapgood and omitting Di Peso and subsequent studies.

Today, the Web is full of sites that exhaustively debate the authenticity of the pieces. *Marcianitos verdes*, a blog written by Mexican Luis Ruiz Noguez and dedicated to debunking all sorts of conspiracy theories and paranormal phenomena, presented an extensive analysis of the facts and statements around the Julsrud figures, describing the collection as a huge fraud. Others besides Swift have produced competing

Above: two "Egyptian" specimens at the Museo Waldemar Julsrud
in Acámbaro. Below: the museum today

(although poorly designed) sites, usually dedicated to biblical
studies and Creationism, that provide all sorts of evidence
for the ancient provenance of these items.

In an e-mail response to an inquiry I made, Swift wrote,
"I know for a fact that they [the Acámbaro dinosaurs] were
not made in the '40s–60s . . . To my knowledge, the area
around Acámbaro is the only place in the world that scien-
tists will not do thermoluminescent testing because it gives
a date too old for the figures: from 1,000 A.D. to 2,500 B.C."[65]

65. Swift, email to the author, December 4, 2009.

Later, to prove the multicultural ancient references of the figurines, Swift flooded me with a list of pre-Columbian transoceanic contact theories: the Anasazi had created "a rock art panel that is Egyptian: rainbow, Anubis dog, hippopotamus, and crocodile"; "In Veracruz, Mexico, at the museum, there are many clay statues of faces of people who look Egyptian including the head dress with the Anak Key. One of the faces is a dead ringer of Queen Nefertiti of Egypt"; the Mayan pyramid of Comacalco has on its walls "drawings of Roman frigates, Chinese junks, and islander ships"; regarding the Olmec heads of Villahermosa, Mexico, "the same identical stone heads—about 30 of them—are along the Nile River in a remote part of the Sudan."[66]

* * *

The forgery of archaeological items is as old as the financial and scientific demand that they generate. In many cases, pieces believed to be authentic and exhibited in archaeological museums have later been proven to be falsifications of previous centuries—and undoubtedly there are many such objects today on display in contemporary museums. In Latin America, artifacts from practically every pre-Columbian culture have been forged, from arrowheads to Olmec heads.[67] In 1890 Francisco P. Moreno, a noted

---

66. Swift, e-mail to the author, December 9, 2009.
67. In 2002, for several million euros a Swiss collector bought an Olmec head that had appeared in an exhibition in Europe. It was later found out through photographic evidence of its fabrication that it was a forgery concocted by a Costa Rican dealer. Julio Aguilar, *"Cabeza olmeca: historia de un fraude,"* El Universal, www.eluniversal.com.mx/cultura/56046.html.

Argentine archaeologist, announced to the astonishment of the archaeology community that he had discovered Aztec ceramic objects in Laguna de los Lobos, on the outskirts of Buenos Aires. Closer examination showed that the pieces were indeed authentic but had actually come from the Valley of Mexico—the Teotihuacán region. As it turned out, Moreno had not visited the putative site but had taken the word of the man who had "found" the pieces, a hacienda owner named Isidro Cieza. Further examination of the area showed no evidence of ancient cultures.

The famous case of the Ica Stones in Peru involved a Julsrud-like collector (Javier Cabrera, a doctor) and a local farmer (Basilio Uschuya), like Odilón. In 1966, for his birthday Cabrera received a stone bearing a carved representation of what appeared to be an ancient fish. He eventually connected with Uschuya, who became his personal supplier of these items. Cabrera collected around fifteen thousand artifacts, some of which had images of dinosaur-like animals. Like the Acámbaro dinosaurs, these images became a fascination for Creationists, and they also attracted theorists of the paranormal, who saw evidence of extraterrestrial cultures in the stones. However, a few years later, when Peruvian authorities arrested Uschuya on a charge of trafficking archaeological items, he confessed that he had forged the pieces and even demonstrated his procedure for television cameras, adding, "Carving stones is easier than farming the land."[68] Nonetheless, and even after these revelations, Cabrera remained unfazed. He agreed

---

68. Basilio Uschuya, quoted in Filip Coppens, "Jurassic Library—The Ica Stones," *Fortean Times Magazine*, October 2001.

that some pieces had indeed been forged but claimed that others were authentic and Uschuya had made a false confession to avoid jail.

As it sometimes happens with hoaxes, in the case of both the Ica Stones and the Julsrud artifacts even the most final proof of their falsity can't fight popular imagination. Believers in the Julsrud artifacts will perhaps never accept even the most crystal-clear proofs of a hoax, and there will always be bloggers and researchers ready to attempt, unsuccessfully, to put the issue to rest once and for all.

Debates about the artifacts spin historical facts, measurements, dating techniques, and materials, none of which seem to have any final resolution. Even when the most definitive scientific proof is given about a hoax, believers always find a crevice or loophole through which to question the findings and allow the myth to survive.

A simple visual analysis of the objects may be the most objective and direct route to the truth—which may indicate why Di Peso did not spend more time with the Julsrud collection when he visited in 1952. For any semi-experienced art viewer, the hoax is immediately and visibly clear—truly, a no-brainer. Compared to authentic pre-Columbian objects, the Julsrud artifacts are an inventive but highly uneven lot. Many of them look like the products of a high school ceramics class. They tend to be whimsical and creative—perhaps if their makers had opened a traditional ceramics shop they would have become popular and successful artisans. But in comparison to authentic Mesoamerican objects, the Julsrud sculptures are mediocre and crude in manufacture, formally indistinct, and lacking unity and the type of cohesiveness that only a collective sense of purpose—that is, a cosmogony—can inscribe. Odilón and his collaborators were able fabricators, but they didn't or couldn't concoct the cultural and religious logic of an entire culture, likely because they were not such sophisticated forgers. In any case, they didn't have to: Mr. Julsrud bought everything they made.

Looking at some of the most audacious representations in the collection, like the woman making out with the alligator, one can't help imagining the great time the Acámbaro families must have had in making them. In an ironic twist of the story, the illiterate Mexican villagers outsmarted the amateur archaeologists, pseudoscientists, and delusional charlatans who thought they had discovered a secret culture. Odilón barely gets any credit in the pro-Julsrud literature, named as a mere facilitator, but he was in fact the mastermind, the artistic director, possibly the artist, and most definitely the one who took the money and ran, and his legacy continues. If history is to be fair, we can only hope that one day the Waldemar Julsrud Museum

will be renamed the Odilón Tinajero Museum of Tourist Scams, or, as some skeptics have suggested, The Museum of the Archaeological Fraud.

Odilón's scheme was a brilliant hoax, but the Julsrud pieces are not too different from the thousands of "pre-Columbian" craft objects for sale outside every archaeological tourist site in Mexico. Every now and then, when visiting one of those sites, I spot a gullible French or American tourist purchasing an item, believing he or she is obtaining a "real" archaeological artifact. Every observant visitor to Mexico is familiar with the extraordinary inventiveness of Mexican artisans, which ranges from

strict imitation of pre-Columbian objects to the invention
of new ones. The production of these types of crafts has
long been a family business, as Di Peso correctly claimed.
In the 1930s, a man named Pedro Linares started his own
tradition, creating fantastic creatures in papier-mâché that
became known as *alebrijes*, inspired by real and mythic
animals. The work of the Linares family is now a staple
of every Mexican folk-art shop. Likewise, the Julsrud collection is nothing other than the very prolific output of a
couple of families—probably those Di Peso found a few
miles away from Julsrud's house.

The real Chupícuaro culture emerged around 400 B.C.,
in the late Preclassic period. Its pottery, which constitutes
some of the oldest artifacts of ancient Mexico, is exquisitely
patterned and elegantly designed and widely considered
to be among the finest in Mesoamerica. Chupícuaro clay

sculptures include representations of families, of lactation, birth, and death. The fertility figurines are mysterious and beautiful, with elongated eyes. They often appear to be smiling, as if satisfied to be keeping their mystery from us, silently reveling in the fact that we, the living mortals, are so profoundly ignorant about the past.

WHO IS WHAT AND WHAT IS WHO

I am a man: little do I last
and the night is enormous.
But I look up:
the stars write.
Unknowing I understand:
I too am written,
and at this very moment
someone spells me out.

—Octavio Paz

HUMAN-MADE OBJECTS are necessarily imperfect; their users, those who interact with them, project perfection onto them in the form of narratives, completing them, as, Marcel Duchamp wrote, a viewer completes a work of art. Humans *have* to have narratives for every object. We are wired to experience the world that way—we have a tendency to resolve ambiguity, to decide, for instance, if an object is more circular than square, even if it is neither. It is our way to assimilate and make sense of reality.

That is the principle Froelich Rainey used to tease his guests in *What in the World?*: they were asked to construct the real story of an anonymous object that had been extracted from its original cultural script. Ironically, even when the "answer" about what the object was had been given or revealed to the panel, the object still often remained fairly obscure (although that didn't seem to matter much for the purposes of the TV show).

The same is true when we analyze and discuss objects in museums. The modalities of object interpretation—formal analysis, theoretical discussion, or simple biographical/ anecdotal storytelling about the object or its author—are all hermeneutic tools that produce valuable and necessary appreciation but never a definitive reading, simply because the nature of interpretation is that very shift of perceptions that affect meaning—the ever-evolving "fusion of horizons" as described by Gadamer.

In the same way we instinctively seek a self-contained story about every object, we also want objects to have some sort of authenticity—a verified connection to a particular valued context or individual. Yet authenticity is an ambiguous concept in its practical use (Maxwell Sommerville's Buddhist temple, for instance, was "authentic," in that all its materials came from Asia, but few people knowing that fact would use that word to describe it) and to this date we haven't entirely figured out how to assimilate this fact in academia and in cultural production. For Martin Heidegger, authenticity is not a crucial concept or even a usefully evaluative one for defining the self—rather, it describes one of several possibilities of being. The growing post-war awareness of the treacherous nature of the notion of authenticity caused it to become a central concern in postmodern art, culminating with the more radical steps taken by conceptual artists to completely eliminate the aura of the original art object. Museums that collect art made after 1960 haven't completely resolved how to deal philosophically with an aesthetic position that challenges their own identities as guardians, or bestowers, of authenticity. For artists like Sol LeWitt and Donald Judd, not touching their works was a central part of the pieces—they were fabricated industrially or by assistants and are repeatable, even after the artists' death—yet we preserve their work religiously, because the original objects are the closest thing we have to the artist's hand and vision. Yet in art and in culture, it is the historical moment that gives meaning to objects—something that is impossible to recreate. As a result, whether conceptual artwork or an ancient archaeological artifact, objects are always the next best thing: they are relics of an original situation that can never recur, much as, Heraclitus wrote, you never can step into the same river twice.

Because of their slippery relationship with narrative closure and authenticity, archaeological artifacts remain mysterious even when we think we know their exact stories and origins. This is because interpretive projections are infinite, affected as they are by the changing social and cultural contexts of interpretation. Therein also lies the core of what Karl Marx meant when he wrote, describing commodity fetishism, that commodities are a mysterious thing. We don't know why some are more compelling than others or predict which will be more or less valuable in the future, as cultural perspectives fluctuate from era to era.

Collectively or individually, we are responsible for giving meaning and value to objects, and as such we operate at home like curators operate in a museum. Psychologists Mihaly Csikszentmihalyi and Eugene Rochberg-Halton made a thorough study of this phenomenon, published in 1981 as *The Meaning of Things*. Csikszentmihalyi interviewed eighty families at their homes in Chicago regarding the value of objects they owned. Most of their objects weren't worth much monetarily, but many of them gave great pleasure, enhancing the lives of their owners and thus accruing personal, symbolic value. In the vast majority of cases, the most meaningful value was not financial but sentimental or anecdotal.[69]

Collectors—or curators in charge of collections—transform the meaning and value of objects and in turn they are transformed by their collections in unsuspecting, sometimes dramatic ways. Louis Shotridge became chief spokesperson for the Tlingit items he collected, such Ghost of Courageous Adventurer, and he was a victim of the protagonic role he had assigned to himself. In response to a simple scam, Waldemar Julsrud dedicated his life to a fictional prehistoric culture, while he inadvertently funded the development of an inventive folk art collection. In the process of losing his sanity while digging for cuneiform tablets, John Henry Haynes's suggestion that he had found a "Temple Library" stimulated the imagination of many to think of these objects as an encyclopedic collection of ancient knowledge, when in reality they were records of scribal exercises. Maxwell Sommerville was so obsessed with his grandiose vision of discovering rare items and Buddhist treasures that he not only fell prey to fictions he had himself constructed but obscured his true museological achievements. In all these cases, the protagonists—collectors, adventurers, and those who followed or opposed them—sought to possess and interpret objects, to control their stories, but in the end it was the objects that narrated their keepers.

In a quiz show, with smoke curtain or not, there is an answer—that is, a closed story—to every question. In

69. Mihaly Csikszentmihalyi and Eugene Rochberg-Halton, *The Meaning of Things: Domestic Symbols and the Self* (Cambridge University Press, Cambridge, UK, 1981) pp. 225–249.

archaeology, as in art, there are nothing but open-ended threads of meaning to every object. And the only authenticity lies in our process of projecting ourselves onto them, as we allow them to spell us out.

BIBLIOGRAPHY

Benson, Diane. "Superficial Treatment of a Sensitive History," *Anchorage Daily News*, July 22, 2001.

Berges, Dietrich. *Antike Siegel und Glasgemmen der Sammlung Maxwell Sommerville*. Mainz am Rhein: Verlag Philipp Von Zabern, 2002.

Board of Managers of the Archaeological Department of the University of Pennsylvania, Letter of acceptance of Hermann Hillprecht's resignation, February 21, 1911. University of Pennsylvania Museum of Archaeology and Anthropology Archives.

Colimore, Edward. "A Shopping Trip She Won't Forget," *Philadephia Inquirer*, October 31, 1991. (news article about the recovery of the crystal ball)

Conn, Steven. *Museums and American Intellectual Life, 1876–1926*. Chicago: University of Chicago Press, 1998.

———. "Going Native for an Afternoon: Maxwell Sommerville, His Buddhist Temple and the Search for a Usable Asia", lecture at Kings College, Cambridge, June 2004 (transcript at University Museum Archives)

Coppens, Filip. "Jurassic Library—The Ica Stones." *Fortean Times*, October 2001.

Csikszentmihalyi, Mihaly, and Eugene Rochberg-Halton. *The Meaning of Things: Domestic Symbols and the Self*. Cambridge: Cambridge University Press, 1981.

Culin, Stuart. "The Professor of Glyptology," unpublished manuscript, n.d. Culin Archival Collection, Brooklyn Museum, New York.

Dauenhauer, Norah Marks. *Ghost of Corageous Adventurer*. In *Native American Voices on Identity, Art and Culture: Objects of Everlasting Value*. Lucy Fowler Williams, William S. Wierzbowski, Robert W. Preucel, editors. Philadelphia: University of Pennsylvania Museum of Archaeology and Anthropology, 2005.

Dessart, George. *"What in the World*: A Television Institution," *Expedition* 4, no. 1 (Fall 1961).

Di Peso, Charles C. "The Clay Figurines of Acámbaro, Guanajuato, Mexico," *American Antiquity* 18, no. 4 (April 1953).

Hapgood, Charles H. *Mystery in Acámbaro*. Winchester, N.H.: Published by the author, 1973.

Harmer, Lowell. "Mexico Finds Give Hint of Lost World," *Los Angeles Times*, March 25, 1951.

Haynes, John Henry. Letters to John Peters, third Nippur campaign, 1893–96. University of Pennsylvania Museum of Archaeology and Anthropology Archives.

"Haynes' Tablet," *North Adams Evening Transcript*, Saturday, December 9, 1916.

Johnson, Eldridge A. Letter to George Byron Gordon, January 4, 1927. University of Pennsylvania Museum of Archaeology and Anthropology Archives.

Jones, Harry Dillon. "Gods, Gems and Mascots: The Life-Work of Maxwell Sommerville," *Booklovers Magazine* 4, no. 1 (July 1904).

Kaplan, Susan A., and Kristin J. Barsness. *Raven's Journey: The World of Alaska's Native People*. Philadelphia: University of Pennsylvania Museum of Archaeology and Anthropology, 1986.

K. E. J., "Americans at Nippur," *Biblical Archaeology Review* 24, no. 6 (November–December 1998).

Kuklick, Bruce. "'My Life's Shattered Work!': The Strange Ordeal of Hermann Hillprecht," *Archaeology Oddyssey*, May/June 2000.

————. *Puritans in Babylon: The Ancient Near East and American Intellectual Life, 1880–1930*. Princeton, N.J.: Princeton University Press, 1996.

Lopez, John S. "The Hoodwinking of American Collectors", *Appleton's Magazine* 9, nos. 1–6 (1907).

Lyons, Elizabeth Maxwell Sommerville biographical narrative, December 1985. University of Pennsylvania Museum of Archaeology and Anthropology Archives.

Madeira, Jr., Percy C. *Men in Search of Man*. Philadelphia: University of Pennsylvania Press, 1964.

Miller, J. Leroy. "A Giant Jewel of China," *Mentor*, January 1929.

"Nippur, narrative of 3rd expedition, second version," 1896, University of Pennsylvania Museum of Archaeology and Anthropology Archives, #230.

Ochsenschlacher, Edward L. *Iraq's Marsh Arabs in the Garden of Eden*. Chapter 14: "The Photographs of John Henry Haynes." Philadelphia: University of Pennsylvania Museum of Archaeology and Anthropology, 2004.

"Penn Museum Crystal Ball, Status Stolen, Guard Ignored Burglar Alarms," *Philadelphia Daily News*, November 12, 1988

Pezzati, Alex. "Mystery at Acámbaro, Mexico," *Expedition* 47, no. 3 (Winter 2005).

————. "Nipper in the Jungle," *Expedition* 47, no. 1 (Spring 2005).

Rostron, Bryan. "Is Science Ahead of the Forger?," *New York Times*, August 19, 1979.

Russell, William N. "Did Man Tame the Dinosaurs?," *Fate*, February–March 1952.

"Sharing Our Knowledge" edited by Sergei Kan and Steve Henrikson; (Currently under review by the University of Nebraska Press).

Shaw, John, *Farang Fables*, City Life Chiang Mai, Vol. 11, No. 10, 2002

Shotridge, Louis. "Ghost of Courageous Adventurer," *Museum Journal* (University of Pennsylvania Museum of Archaeology and Anthropology), Vol. 11, 1920.

———. "My Northland Revisited," *Museum Journal* (University of Pennsylvania Museum of Archaeology and Anthropology), Vol. 8, 1917.

Sommerville, Maxwell. *Monograph of the Buddhist Temple of the Free Museum of Science and Art*. Exhibition brochure. Philadelphia: University of Pennsylvania Museum of Archaeology and Anthropology, 1904.

———. *Engraved Gems: Their History and an Elaborate View of Their Place in Art*. Philadelphia: Published by the author, 1889.

Statterwhite, Lytton. Ephemera for the exhibition *Old Stone-Age or Modern Comic-Book Art?*, winter 1955–56. University of Pennsylvania Museum of Archaeology and Anthropology Archives, American section, Julsrud Coll.

Urminska, Suzanna A. "The Ethnographic Photography of Louis Shotridge," unpublished manuscript, 2001. University of Pennsylvania Museum of Archaeology and Anthropology Archives.

Vermeule, Cornelius C. *Cameo and Intaglio: Engraved Gems from the Sommerville Collection*. Philadelphia: University of Pennsylvania Museum of Archaeology and Anthropology, 1956.

Williams, Lucy Fowler. *Louis Shotridge: Preserver of Tlingit History*. 2009.

Witte, William. Interview by J. A. Mason, July 26, 1953. University of Pennsylvania Museum of Archaeology and Anthropology Archives.

Photo Credits

pp. *iii*, 17, Pablo Helguera.

pp. *v*, 93, 96, 100, 104, Photos from Charles Hapgood's Mystery in Acambaro, 1973.

p. 1, Penn Museum image 23366. View of the Warden Garden at the University of Pennsylvania Museum of Archaeology and Anthropology. Photograph by Karl F. Lutz, c. 1964.

p. 7, Penn Museum image 56188. WCAU personnel creating a smoke effect with dry ice for the "What in the World?" television show. Photographed at WCAU TV Studios, c. 1960.

p. 14, Penn Museum image 139460. Carleton Coon, Jacques Lipchitz, and Alfred Kidder II, study an object, while Froelich Rainey moderates the "What in the World?" television show. Photographed at WCAU TV Studios, c. 1960.

p. 23, Penn Museum image 152271. Painting of Maxwell Sommerville (1829–1904). Oil on canvas. Pictured with pieces of gem collection, collected Buddhist Art and classical engraved gems.

p. 24, *Appleton's Magazine*, 1907.

p. 26, Penn Museum image 9618. Portrait of Maxwell Sommerville as athlete.

p. 27, Maxwell Sommerville, from *The Booklovers Magazine* vol. 4 no. 1 July 1904.

p. 31, Penn Museum image 175434. "Within the Chancel Rail." Maxwell Sommerville dressed in Buddhist robes in his Buddhist temple exhibit, from *Monograph of the Buddhist Temple* by Peirce & Jones.

pp. 39, 114, 115, photos wikimedia commons.

p. 43, Penn Museum image 139049. View of excavations of Temple enclosure as seen from top of Ziggurat at Nippur in Iraq. Photograph by John Henry Haynes, August 15, 1899.

p. 46, Hermann Vollrath Hilprecht (Library of Congress).

p. 47, Penn Museum image 139034. John Punnett Peters (1852-1921).

p. 50, Penn Museum image 149706. Portrait of John Henry Haynes (1849-1910), c. 1900, business.

p. 54, Penn Museum image 143996. Watercourse revealed by excavations at Nippur. Workers carry away baskets of dirt. Photograph by John Henry Haynes, 1895.

p. 56, Joseph A. Meyer, Jr., (seated) with fellow students in the Architecture Library of the Massachusetts Institute of Technology, ca. 1887-91. Massachusetts Institute of Technology Museum.

p. 63, Penn Museum image 14857. Musicians participating in funeral ceremonies—Frog House and Salmon House. Photograph by Louis Shotridge.

p. 64, Penn Museum image 151891, object NA8488. Tlingit dagger with skull-decorated handle, made of iron and ivory, called "Ghost of Courageous Adventurer." From the Klukwan Dagisdinaa Clan, Thunder House. Early 19th century. Length—38.6 cm. Photograph by Karen Mauch and John Chew, 2003.

p. 66, Penn Museum image 140236. Portrait of Louis Shotridge at the Penn Museum. Shotridge is dressed in materials from the Heye Collection. Photograph by William Witte, February 1912.

p. 68, Penn Museum image 11820. George Byron Gordon and canoe, c. 1907.

p. 70, Penn Museum image 15111. Figure with sled dogs on Chilkat River. Photograph by Louis Shotridge, March 1923.

p. 73, Penn Museum image 14848. "After the first snow, and no snowshoes." Louis Shotridge standing in the snow.

p. 81, Penn Museum objects C681A and C681B. Crystal Ball of the "Empress Dowager" Tz'u Hsi, resting on a silver base in the form of a wave.

p. 82, Empress Dowager Cixi (Library of Congress).

p. 85, Penn Museum image 19136. Portrait of George Byron Gordon.

p. 89, Penn Museum image 183125:08. Two girls looking at crystal sphere in Harrison Rotunda antechamber. Crystal ball of the "Empress Dowager" Tz'u Hsi, resting on a silver base in the form of a wave. Photograph by Reuben Goldberg, 1954.

p. 97, Penn Museum image 184513. Ceramic figurine from the Waldemar Julsrud collection, Acambaro, Mexico. Photograph c. 1955.

pp. 98, 99, 109, 113, Photo Esteban Reyes.

p. 117, Nevil Gallery for The Blind and Sighted, Penn Museum, Philadelphia, 1980.

Acknowledgments

This book is the result of an exhibition project. José Ignacio Roca, artistic director of Philagrafika, invited me to the University Museum, and the resulting exhibition at the Museum and this book could not have been envisioned without him. Bill Wierzbowski, Associate Keeper of the American Collection at the museum, was a central supporter of and participant in the research and implementation of this project. He was an absolutely irreplaceable, patient, good-humored and unflinchingly supportive guide in my logistical and administrative wanderings through the museum—I would have been lost without him. Similarly, I am indebted to Alex Pezzati, director of the museum's archive and true keeper of its stories, whose memory, knowledge and helpfulness made my research not only productive but enormously enjoyable. I am most grateful to the director of the University Museum, Dr. Richard Hodges, as well as the museum's chief of staff and head of collections, James R. Mathieu, who generously and enthusiastically opened the doors of the museum and the institution's resources to allow me peek into its history and create this unauthorized biography of sorts. I am well aware of the trepidation that the presence of an outside observer can cause in an institution, and this makes me even more appreciative that I was made to feel welcome to open every closet in the museum to look for skeletons. The entire staff of the museum went beyond the call of duty, submitting to interviews, assisting with research, and answering questions. They included Chrisso Boulis, Registrar; Lucy Fowler Williams, Keeper of the American Section; and Philip Jones, Associate Curator of the Babylonian Section. Kate Quinn, the exhibitions designer and her talented team including Aaron Billheimer, Matt Applebaum, and Ben Neiditz worked around the clock to make the exhibition possible. I am similarly grateful to Loa Traxtler, Pam Kosty, Maureen Callahan, and Amy Ellsworth, who provided invaluable help in conducting staff interviews.

I am thankful for the support of Wendy Woon, Deputy Director of Education at the Museum of Modern Art, and that of my colleagues in the Department of Education there—my interlocutors and my inspiration on ideas of audiences and interpretation. Caitlin Perkins, of Philagrafika, was a most reliable and helpful support for this project and made sure it moved forward whenever it was stuck. Esteban Reyes was a key collaborator, venturing to Acámbaro to gather information and materials.

I am grateful as always to Jorge Pinto, who supported the publication of this book, to the ever-precise editing of Rebecca Roberts and the painstaking design of Charles King, and for the always key support of my assistant Jeff Eaton, who traveled to Philadelphia with me to do research and helped in every step of the way. Last, but not least, I am always in debt to my wife, Dannielle Tegeder, who supports my work, and to our new daughter Estela, who made sure I woke up every morning at 5 a.m. to feed her and fit my daily page or two of archaeological biographies.

About the Author

Pablo Helguera (born in Mexico City, 1971) is a visual and performance artist. Past art projects have included a phonographic archive of dying languages, a memory theater, fourteen visual artist "heteronyms," and four fictional opera composers. Helguera is the author of eight books, including *The Pablo Helguera Manual of Contemporary Art Style* (2005, English version 2007), *The Witches of Tepoztlán (and Other Unpublished Operas)* (2007), the novel *The Boy Inside the Letter* (2008), *Artoons I* and *II* (2009), the play *The Juvenal Players* (2009), and the anthology of performance texts *Theatrum Anatomicum (and other Performance Lectures)* (2009). In 2008 he received a Guggenheim Fellowship. In 2006 he drove from Anchorage to Tierra del Fuego with a collapsible schoolhouse, organizing discussions, activist happenings, and civic ceremonies along the way (*The School of Panamerican Unrest*). Helguera is Director of Adult and Academic Programs in the Department of Education at the Museum of Modern Art, New York. He lives in Brooklyn with his wife, Dannielle Tegeder, their daughter, Estela, and their cat, Ceniza.